DEVON
Yarns

Christina Green

D1471562

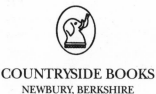

COUNTRYSIDE BOOKS
NEWBURY, BERKSHIRE

First Published 1995
© Christina Green 1995

All rights reserved
No reproduction permitted
without the prior permission
of the publishers:

COUNTRYSIDE BOOKS
3 Catherine Road
Newbury, Berkshire

ISBN 1 85306 334 7

Illustrations by Eve Dymond-White

Designed by Mon Mohan
Produced through MRM Associates Ltd., Reading
Typeset by Textype Typesetters, Cambridge
Printed by Woolnough Bookbinding Ltd., Irthlingborough

Contents

(Continued on page 6)

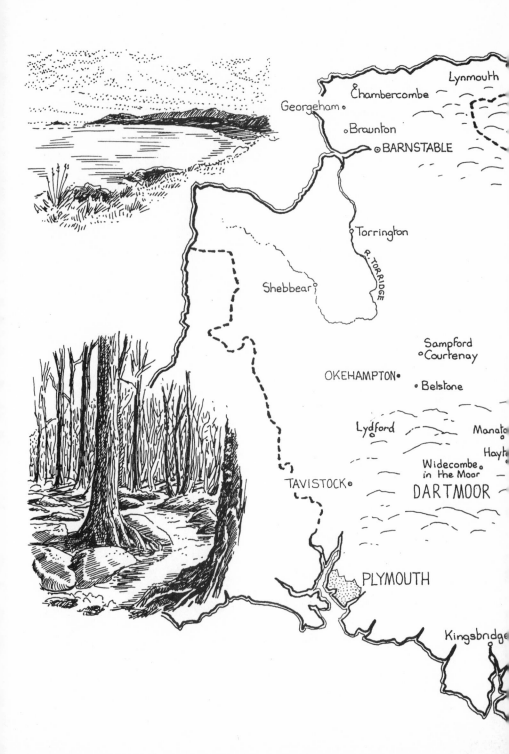

Lynmouth

Chambercombe

Georgeham

Braunton

BARNSTABLE

Torrington

R. TORRIDGE

Shebbear

Sampford
Courtenay

OKEHAMPTON

Belstone

Lydford

Manato

Hayt

Widecombe
in the Moor

TAVISTOCK

DARTMOOR

PLYMOUTH

Kingsbridge

EXMOOR

TIVERTON

BLACKDOWN
HILLS

Membury

HONITON
Gittisham

CREDITON

Uplyme

EXETER

Axmouth

Lyme
Regis

Hennock

Bovey
Tracey

Exmouth

ewton
bbot

Teignmouth

Berry
Pomeroy

OTNES

SLAPTON
SANDS

1

Mary Jay Lives On

How strange, say visitors to Dartmoor, as they come upon the small, turfed mound that lies beside the road running from Hound Tor to Beetor Cross – a grave! Whose is it? And why is it here – by the road?

The story of Mary – sometimes, for unknown reasons, called Kitty – Jay, has evolved over the centuries, marrying fact and romantic fiction into an enduring legend. The tale, as told today, is a sad one, but not unusual, starting as it does with a dead woman's baby being taken in by the local Poor House in Newton Abbot in or around 1790. According to custom, the abandoned scrap was given a surname beginning with the alphabetical letter currently in use in the institution. All the Jacksons, Joneses and Jeffereys were already named, so this newcomer was called simply 'Jay'. But said a scandalised official, 'that be slang for prostitute . . .' So little Jay was given the christian name of Mary as a redeeming hope for her future.

Mary Jay stayed at the Poor House well into her teens, kept long after the customary age of six or seven, when orphaned boys and girls were normally sent out to earn their livings as apprentices. Perhaps she was more biddable and easily put upon than her companions; whatever the reason, she remained at Wolborough Poor House, helping to supervise the younger children.

She was in her teens when, finally, she was packed off to live with a farming family on the eastern side of Dartmoor, not far from the village of Manaton. What could have been her thoughts as she carried her box of scant belongings to the Magistrate's house, where her master-to-be waited to sign the indenture undertaking to employ her? Excitement, perhaps, at escaping from the restrictive and tedious life that was all she had ever known. And possibly a certain fear at what might lie before her. But, whatever emotions filled her that morning, Mary Jay could have had no inkling of her true destiny.

The wild grandeur and solitude of the moor kept her silent, jogging along, riding pillion on her master's horse. After years of living within the four walls of the institution, with only limited exercise in the town itself, this boundless landscape was a revelation. Granite tors frowned down upon the surrounding waste, bracken grew tall and rivers sang and gleamed in the windy sunshine, as the narrow, winding lane bore Mary Jay ever nearer to her new home.

The old farm on the outskirts of Manaton was built of stone, as tough and unforgiving as the moor itself. In those days, apprentices such as Mary Jay were given tasks both in the house and fields that often demanded much greater physical effort and endurance than they possessed. Consequently, accounts of the time tell us that beatings and harsh treatment were common. Some children slept three to a bed, were frequently half-starved and given only hand-me-down clothes from the ragbag to protect them from the severe cold and wet of the cruel moorland weather. Days began before dawn, with getting in the cows, feeding and then milking them before tending the pigs. Boy apprentices were expected to work as hard as grown labourers, although young dairymaids had a slightly easier time. In most households the normal regime was relentlessly harsh, with little reward save the apprentice's keep. And girls were often abused by both masters and their sons.

Yet – who knows? – perhaps even this sort of existence offered a meagre warmth and security, both so sadly missing from a Poor House child's life. Despite her indifferent treatment and the wearisome demands of the work, maybe Mary found a degree of content, living and working within a small family community, no longer part of an impersonal and ever-shifting institution. Small wonder, then, if as she settled slowly down some of her natural shyness and timidity left her. It might well be here that her name was changed to Kitty, which is how she was remembered in the early 1900s. When the son of the family favoured her with his attentions, perhaps Mary gave herself freely, naïvely thinking that this was the first step to becoming a real member of a family – for the first time in her short life.

One can only imagine the girl's feelings when she discovered she was pregnant, and a heart-rending scene must have followed when she told her lover the news. What happened then is any-one's guess, but the outcome was inevitable.

Mary Jay was angrily reminded that she was only a girl from the Poor House and that she had lived up to the meaning of her ill-chosen name – why, of course, she had thrown herself at the young master. And she must leave the house now – NOW! This very minute . . .

Where could she go? Back to Wolborough, facing disgrace and even greater chastisement? Should she have the child and find another employer? But even Mary Jay, in her innocence, must have realised that gossip would irrevocably brand her a slut. No respectable farmer would ever consider taking her on after this. A single mother, in those times, was instantly consigned to the dregs of society, and left to survive as best she could. And many did not.

So Mary Jay, in utter despair, hanged herself in the barn of her employer's farm at Canna, thus ending the sad story. Yet it does not finish there, for now, more than 200 years later, her grave has become one of the most famous, sought-out places on Dartmoor.

According to the dogmatic custom of the times, she was buried in unconsecrated ground at the boundary of three parishes, none of them wishing to own such a reprobate. It is not known if a stake pierced the body – a tradition often carried out to stop the unquiet spirit returning to the place of its death.

The sad little mound beside the track was, from then on, referred to as 'naught but a daid sheep', and might well have been quite forgotten, as it sank deeper into the surrounding turf, had not a local landowner, a Mr James Bryant of nearby Hedge Barton, had the mound dug up and the bones exhumed. They were identified as belonging to a young woman, and he put them in a box, reburying them with a reverence poor Mary never encountered in her life, and setting a granite stone at the head of the newly-turfed grave. In the 1970s the Dartmoor National Park Authority kerbed the grave with a stone surround to protect it from wandering cattle.

There she lies still. And, in the manner of folklore, the few known facts have been added to, subtracted from and thickly embroidered, until the tale has become a living legend.

Some years ago it was noticed that flowers were appearing on the grave. Curious watchers saw no one put them there. At night, it was said, the grave was bare, but dawn would find a posy of seasonal blooms – foxgloves, gorse, heather, fern, holly or ivy – lying on the wet grass. Gossip suggested that Beatrice Chase, a local authoress living at Widecombe, had been the first to honour the poor maid with flowers. But if that was the case, who kept up the practice after Beatrice died? Pixies were hinted at, the little mischievous folk of Dartmoor, seldom seen, but known to have fingers in many pies. Today the practice continues, carried out by human hands, as each casual passer-by, or sympathetic mourner searching out the grave, offers up a few flowers.

For many years now the grave has become the centre of fascinated activity. There are stories of local haunting parties visiting it, chancing upon each other, sheet-draped and howling in the mysterious moorland darkness, and frightening themselves half to death; a rare touch of mirth in the canon of tales surrounding this unhappy legend.

A novel has been written about Mary Jay's life, and some tender, evocative poetry. In 1978 a north-country woman who had never heard of Mary Jay, or of Manaton, appeared on television, submitting to hypnosis, during which she relived the short tragic life. Afterwards she mentioned places and characters of which she knew nothing in conscious life.

Lately, coins have been found on the grave. Clearly it has now become a form of wishing well – or a begging bowl. And sometimes there are pathetic little notes, slipped beneath the bunches of flowers decorating the turf. They wish Mary Jay well and even thank her for giving solace to the writers.

How sad it is to reflect that, alive, poor little Mary found herself completely alone, while now, dead and buried, it seems the whole world has become her friend and admirer.

2

Louisa to the Rescue

The Royal Naval Lifeboat Institution is a voluntary organisation which, since its foundation in 1824, has rescued many thousands of people.

Lifeboatmen and women come from all walks of life, and voluntarily commit themselves to leaving their homes before, after or during their day's work, to answer distress calls. When they put to sea, they face fatigue, the cold and wet, and, despite the power of modern lifeboats designed to the highest standards and fitted with sophisticated equipment, possible danger. This tale of the launching of the *Louisa* at Lynmouth, North Devon, in 1899, vividly illustrates the bravery, stamina and dedication of lifeboat crews.

The North Devon coast, composed of some of the highest cliffs in the country, is spectacular but hazardous. It has been a graveyard of wrecked ships since the first settlers, in their tiny, wind-powered boats, arrived there 4,000 years ago. The Bristol Channel appears a sun-touched stretch of placid water one minute, but can very soon become turbulent and highly dangerous. The result of this ever-present threat to men's lives prompted the lifeboat crew of Lynmouth, on that particular stormy evening, to undertake the maddest yet most courageous journey possible.

The story of how the 34 ft long wooden lifeboat, *Louisa*, was pulled 1,300 ft above sea level up a stony, narrow track, manhandled across rough moorland in a howling gale in the darkness, and then somehow manoeuvred down deadly Porlock Hill to be finally launched for a sea-rescue, is in the heroic mould. Often told, it can stand yet another telling, because of the courage and vision of the ordinary men who took part in it.

Seven pm on 12th January 1899. As the north-west wind increased to severe gale force, messages were received that a large ship was drifting ashore and sending up distress signals. Watchers along the coast at Lynmouth, Minehead and Porlock Weir, with their lack of modern-day technology, could not know the true situation, that the 1900 ton *Forest Hall*'s towline to the accompanying tug, the *Joliffe*, had parted in the storm. The tug, seeing *Forest Hall* put down two anchors, stood off, waiting for the gale to abate. There were 18 men aboard and the ship was being towed to its home port of Liverpool. As a result of the tug line severing, the *Forest Hall* lost her steering gear and began drifting helplessly, at the mercy of the gale, the tide carrying her ever nearer to the back-breaking rocky coast. Yet the tug, lying close by, was her insurance and, should the worst happen, would be her rescuer.

But in Minehead and Lynmouth, where telegrams were exchanged, the situation appeared desperate, and the decision

was taken to launch a lifeboat to go to her aid. Watchet could not launch, and neither could Lynmouth, as the harbour was full and flooding.

At Lynmouth the crew of the *Louisa* consulted. It was the second coxswain, young W.R. Richards, who conceived the idea of taking the boat to Porlock Weir, 13 miles up-coast, and launching her there. There must have been a moment's startled silence as he made the extraordinary suggestion, and then the voices crowded across each other – impossible! Crazy! And yet . . . In the light of sober discussion it finally appeared the only thing to do. Yes, they would try.

They called on two experienced stagecoach drivers, Tom Willis, who came down from nearby Lynton with a dozen horses from his stables, along with his colleague, William Vellacott. Questions arose. How many horses would be needed – 15–20? And surely a cart must be sent up the hill first, with tools to clear the way where necessary? In the frequent retelling of this tale no mention has been made of the families of the determined men, but of course they were there, the women putting on brave faces as they rounded up the children and other helpers to make great pots of tea before the crew embarked on its long, life-saving journey.

At eight in the evening, with the *Louisa* lashed to a wheeled carriage, horses harnessed in front, and the majority of men pushing from behind, the procession slowly left Lynmouth and, in howling wind, rain and darkness, only feebly lit by flickering oil lamps, started the ascent of mile-long, 4-in-1, Countisbury Hill. The horses slid and stumbled their way upward, slowly taking the enormous strain of the wooden boat on its swaying carriage.

The men were soon drenched to the skin, their hands made clumsy by the force of the wind, but they were determined. At one point a wheel of the carriage came off. It was repaired and again the horses took the strain, snorting and champing as they climbed ever upward. At the top of the hill the moor awaited them. Ashton Gate and County Gate had to be navigated, with posts being removed. Then a new method of transport had to be tackled, for the carriage wheels would not run over heather and scrub, so small skids, used at times to launch the boat over a low-tide beach, were put in position. Inch by inch, the men heaved at the ropes, moving the skids innumerable times before the rough patch was conquered, and the boat was able to join the carriage, which had been driven separately to the road leading down into Porlock.

Porlock Hill posed another hazard. Corkscrew bends combined with drops of 1-in-4 made this a hill used in the early days of motoring, to test out the brakes of manufacturers' coaches and cars. Somehow the crew of the *Louisa* manhandled their load down its dark, tortuous labyrinth.

The horses were unharnessed, the boat lashed more firmly to the carriage, and the men took up the strain with their own strength, ropes and chains being used as drags to lessen the enormous pull of the descent. Entering Porlock village, they found a cottage obstructing them. They demolished one wall, despite the clamour of the old lady living inside it. Next they discovered that part of the road to Porlock Weir had been washed away. Another delay while trees were lopped along the higher road. But they reached their destination safely at last. It was six in the morning and the men had already laboured unceasingly for the last ten hours – on top of the previous day's work. Yet the *Louisa* was launched, reaching the *Forest Hall* at 7.30 am.

Explanations then revealed the actual situation. The damaged *Joliffe* had put into port for repairs, and then rejoined the *Forest Hall*, making contact with the *Louisa* as she came alongside. Half of the crew of the lifeboat went aboard to help handle her, for the gale still blew. Eventually all three vessels made a safe anchorage in Barry, South Wales, by the evening, where the crew of the *Louisa* ate a large meal together and then had a night's rest. Next morning, with the help of a tow from the *Joliffe*, the *Louisa* returned to Lynmouth. The amazing expedition was over.

Reports vary as to the reception given the crew in Lynmouth. One version of the story insists they were given a tumultuous welcome. Yet, says Jim Butcher, in his *Lifeboat In The Sky*, 'There is no record of a heroes' welcome.' But surely the families, at least, of the men would have been lining the quays, eager to bear them home, there to feed them, warm them, and cherish their bravery.

The *Forest Hall* was repaired and sailed once more, for its original destination, Genoa. The men of the *Louisa* all reported to their respective jobs on Monday morning. In due course each man received a £5 reward, and W.R. Richards, the 16 year old second coxswain, whose heroic idea had set the rescue operation in motion, was given a silver watch, inscribed:

> Presented to
> W.R. Richards
> by R.H. Fry
> for Lifeboat Services, January 1899.

Of course, dull practicalities must, inevitably, follow even the greatest of epic stories. The hire of horses and repairs to the demolished cottage wall amounted to £118 17s 9d. To which the owners of the *Forest Hall* graciously contributed £75.

3

A Person from Hennock

Snow fell thickly on Thursday evening, 8th January 1646 as a dark-cloaked, travel-stained man knocked at a cottage door on the outskirts of Bovey Tracey. He enquired of the occupant, a man named Coniam, where the Presbyterian meeting-house was and when services were held. Believing the caller to be an itinerant preacher, Coniam pulled on his own thick woollen cloak and accompanied his visitor to the village.

At the Presbyterian chapel at the bottom of Hind Street, Coniam and his companion sat through the service, afterwards engaging the elders in conversation. Forgetting that it was wartime with spies infiltrating every gathering, the men talked freely of the Royalist troops in the village. Indeed, they told the quiet, keenly-attentive stranger, amongst other snippets of news, that Wentworth's Rabble – the Royalist officers quartered nearby on the Heathfield – spent their evenings in the Manor House by the river, further down the village, drinking, dicing and wenching.

Five regiments of Lord Wentworth's brigade of horse and foot had been quartered on the Heathfield in the autumn of 1645. Derisively called the Rabble, these officers were savage and undisciplined in their behaviour, plundering the countryside without consideration for lives or property. Lord Wentworth clearly believed his men safely dug-in for the winter, and was disinclined to make any move against the Parliamentarian enemy until spring. The roads were atrocious, the weather severe – no doubt the Royalists felt safely out of harm's way here, in quiet little Bovey Tracey.

The quarters on the Heathfield stretched from Drumbridges, where the Colours were kept, through the heathland and reaching fields near Little Bovey, with a newly-dug breastwork of some 15 ft in height built to protect the village from the south-east, its most vulnerable point of attack. Besides accommodating the man and horsepower of five regiments, there were facilities for stores, transport, and a certain amount of rough social life. Cattle, wagons, work-huts, stables and smithies all rubbed shoulders on the Heathfield during that extremely cold winter. And the inevitable camp followers lived in hastily erected ramshackle buildings, making the camp a snug little world of its own, totally unprepared for attack.

The following year, 1646, was to see the end of the first English Civil War, with the Parliamentary New Model Army, under the control of Oliver Cromwell, sweeping the king's men before it into the south-west of England, and finally beyond, into the toe of Cornwall and on to the Isles of Scilly. It was the end of four years of brutality, unknown since medieval days, and heralded the beginning of a new regime of Puritanical government that was to last for the next eleven years.

The decisive battle of Naseby on 14th June 1645 had provided the impetus to engage on this last sweep of the war, resulting in the New Model Army heading south-west with Colonel Sir Thomas Fairfax in command, and Oliver Cromwell acting as his Lieutenant of Horse.

Dorchester, Yeovil and Bridgwater fell to the newly-disciplined force of the army, affording it vital extra supplies of stores and ammunition. Bristol was successfully stormed, and Exeter besieged, as the Parliamentary troops advanced. They established a secure line of defence, running from Tiverton to Ashton in the Teign valley, these outposts allowing them to continue harrassing and blockading the king's men in walled-up Exeter.

No doubt this was all included in the Presbyterian elders' gossip with Coniam and the stranger. As the evening ended, the man gravely thanked them for their friendly reception, and went out into the stormy night, returning from where he had come – the rough track leading up to the small village of Hennock.

Unknown to the villagers, Parliamentary troops had recently marched from Crediton and were now poised for attack in the

hills above Bovey. Acting on the stranger's information, the next evening, at dusk, the New Model Army swept down into Bovey, taking the Rabble by surprise. They entered the village from the Moretonhampstead road, passing beneath the old arch, a relic of an ancient priory, now called Cromwell's Arch. The troopers halted at the river bridge, where the Royalists were gambling in an upstairs room of the Manor House.

Amid the chaos of attacking horses and men, some of the officers retained enough wit to throw their gambling stakes out of the window, thus hindering the troopers who greedily scrambled for the coins. Escape was possible then, across the river and back to the Heathfield. But the end was irrevocable. Fairfax's men stormed the quarters and a desperate skirmish followed, in which the Royalists were routed. They suffered great losses, including 400 horses and 7 Colours, one of them the Royal Standard itself, emblazoned with King Charles's initials. A bag of 4 colonels, 3

lieutenant-colonels, 5 majors, 11 captains and other officers, 300 arms, 140 prisoners and 150 head of cattle, together with a store of provisions destined for the relief of beseiged Exeter, brought Fairfax a victorious prize.

After the skirmish, Fairfax returned to Moretonhampstead, where Cromwell was now lodging. When news reached him that some 120 Royalists had sought sanctuary at Ilsington church, on the fringe of the moor, a command of horse and foot went after them. The Parliamentarians then marched on to Ashburton, which the majority of fleeing Royalists had occupied the previous night. There is a plaque on the door of what was then the Mermaid Inn – 'General Fairfax lodged here after driving Royalists out on January 10th, 1646.'

Those of the king's followers who survived these local routs fled down into Cornwall, the last stronghold of the Royalist cause, and very shortly the Civil War came to its grim conclusion.

The Heathfield today is partly occupied by an ever-growing industrial estate where roads named Cannon, Cavalier, Roundhead and Musket remind the passer-by of larger issues than the cut and thrust of business. The old breastwork still stands high over the remaining hillocks and ditches of the battlefield, and is surmounted by a rough wooden cross, erected in recent years by the men of the Sealed Knot, a company of the English Civil War Society. The Sealed Knot derives its name from the undercover insignia of men who continued to support the king's cause after Charles I's execution. A plaque at the foot of this cross is inscribed, 'In Memory of the King's Men who fell here Jan 9th, 1645.' The discrepancy in dates is due to the changeover to the Gregorian calendar in 1752, when eleven days were 'lost'.

A redeeming story is still told in Bovey Tracey today, arising from the bitter skirmish. One of the Royalist officers of Wentworth's Rabble was the exception that proves the rule – a kindly, friendly man, well thought of in the village during his stay on the Heathfield. Killed by invading troopers on the old Challacombe Heath, his body was recovered by Fairfax's men who returned to bury the dead of both sides the next day, and a convenient granite longstone was later placed at the head of his grave.

The stone was removed years later, seemingly lost, until it turned up in use as a gatepost at a nearby farm. In 1923 a local man, A.J. Wyatt, re-erected it upon the public footpath that approaches Challabrook Farm. Today the stone stands beside the grassy track, a reminder of the brutal past of Bovey's history, 'This old cross once marked the grave of a Royalist Officer who fell near here in 1645 when Cromwell's troops defeated the Royalists'.

Nowadays, the motorists streaming down the nearby Bovey Straight, or the parallel Old Newton Road, right through the centre of the Heathfield, do not realise that they are driving through a small amphitheatre of war, where the bloody carnage of men and horses stained the snow scarlet, some 350 years ago.

But the memory of that person who trudged down from Hennock to gather vital information—Oliver Cromwell himself—is retained for all time in local folklore.

4

Black Dogs

In 1963, some visitors, en route to the Black Dog Inn near Uplyme, just within the Devon/Dorset border, saw a black dog float out of the hedge ahead of them, at eye level. It continued across the lane – long known as Dog Lane – and then disappeared into the opposite hedge.

No doubt the name of the inn was already fixed in their minds, but can that alone explain such a fascinating sighting? Like all other ghost stories or inexplicable experiences, one only ever hears part of the fantastic tale. But in this case there is a background of similar sightings to be considered.

The apparition first appeared in the early 1800s, when a farmer, living locally, was regularly visited by a ghostly large black dog. Man and beast shared the fire, until mocking comments from his friends made the farmer decide he had had enough of the strange visitations. He attacked the dog, no doubt happily dozing in the warmth of the hearth, with a poker. Instantly, the dog leaped upwards, making a hole in the low ceiling. Gold and silver fell out, enough coins for the astonished man to buy the cottage across the road and go into the hostelry business. Thus did the Black Dog Inn come into being.

In another sighting a local woman reported in 1856 that the dog, when she saw it, grew bigger and bigger, until it turned into a huge cloud, which then vanished. Her less-perceptive husband noticed only incoming sea-mist.

And so the famous 'Black Dog of Devon' has gathered around it a cocoon of weird tales, all slightly different, yet each emphasising the belief that the black dog has always been at large – and still is.

In 1967 a Sticklepath inhabitant told a tale of the owner of a black labrador dog, who, walking past Okehampton Castle grounds, watched his pet suddenly halt, feet stiffly planted and hackles up. The dog would go no further. This spot, said the observer, was precisely the place where, 50 years earlier, she had seen a huge black dog, as large as a pony, jump out of the grounds and stand glaring at her and her small daughter, who was seated on a pet donkey. Even after the dog had disappeared, the donkey refused to pass the spot where the apparition had appeared.

A coincidence perhaps? But Okehampton Castle is the site of a very famous and still current belief in a particular black dog. For this is the destination of notorious 17th-century Lady Howard, who is said to drive there every night across the moor from Tavistock, and back. She rides in a coach made from the bleached bones of her two late husbands. The coachman has no head and the coach is preceded by an enormous black dog with flaming eyes. Occasionally she drives the coach alone, but always with the dog as protector. The legend has many variations, but the image of the black dog persists.

Other black dogs – or is it always the same one? – have been seen on other ancient roads and trackways. Could they be phantoms, still running protectively alongside coaches, wagons and carts no longer visible to the human eye? But if they are reassuringly protective, why does folk memory emphasise the danger of meeting one? See a black dog, ran the old warning, and you'll be dead within the year.

The Hound of the Baskervilles, that monster dog created by Arthur Conan Doyle, who stayed on Dartmoor and so learned of the local superstition, was probably a black dog turned into a highly saleable commodity. Was Conan Doyle also aware of the ancient belief that the black dog is known as the guardian to other levels of consciousness? If so, he couldn't have chosen a better symbol with which to entrance readers who enjoyed being half-scared to death.

Another historical aspect of the black dog is as 'Watchman of the Bridge'. According to a 12th-century writer, mortar mixed with a black dog's blood was used to secure the foundations of bridges. Our pagan ancestors knew all about appeasing their nature gods, and animal sacrifices were made when new buildings were erected, and also at crossroads. Bridges and interconnecting tracks were considered divisions between two worlds; here a door was opened, creating a magical and fearful place. The gods were propitiated with a sacrifice – often a black dog.

Folklore reports at least 50 sightings of these intriguing spectres in Devon in the recorded past. A contemporary collector of black dog stories has theorised that there is an unwavering course along the ancient road north-west of Copplestone, which is 2 miles from Crediton. The road heads for Great Torrington, and sightings have been recorded at Down St Mary, Stopgate Cross and the priory ruins at Frithelstock. The fact that Copplestone Cross is on a Saxon trackway, with a Celtic – decorated granite pillar, is vital to the theory. Further along the haunted route a ditch, the remains of another old track, adds to the historical factors seeming to affect the black dog's journeying. Could the apparition be following one of those mysterious lines of energy, powerful yet hidden beneath the earth, known as ley lines?

But whether the black dog is energy-motivated or just plain ghost-like, sightings are full of fascinating detail. When the dog rushed through Down St Mary, its baying increased as it passed the village smithy. It knocked down part of the schoolhouse, but although stones could be heard crashing to the ground, said the observer, no damage was to be seen when the building was later inspected.

And near Stopgate Cross, a carter, again travelling by night, would always walk at his horse's head, as the dog kept pace with him. He said he felt no fear, despite the size of the creature, but added that he would not try to either touch or speak to it. No one, however, cares to talk about the black dog in St Giles in the Wood, reports of any evidence of its passing being quickly concealed. Yet one woman was heard to admit – after leaving the area – that the dog was always there, and everyone knew about it. It was seen in the area in the 1930s, but since then has been satisfactorily banished from the village consciousness.

But, in 1932, a sighting near Torridge would suggest that the dog was still travelling, for a driver was forced to brake hard one night when he saw a large black dog jump in front of his head-lights. He feared he had hit the creature – it looked real – but he found nothing and saw no sign of it, although the road, both in front and behind him, was clear. The added factors of a steep cliff on one side of the road and a fast-flowing river on the other only emphasised the apparently paranormal character of the animal.

We also hear of sightings on Dartmoor. A black dog was seen by a local farmer's grandfather near Liverton, on the eastern fringe of the moor. The size of a young calf, it walked on its hind legs beside the hedge, he said, panicking the pony he was driving and making it bolt. This was reported by the late folklorist Theo Brown, in 1978, and she also told of another bewildering account which came from a lady who saw not one, but three black dogs passing through her bedroom in the middle of the night. They were completely black, she said, of medium height, and had pointed noses. They brought with them, even in the short period of time she saw them, an uneasy atmosphere, and she admitted to remaining in dread of seeing them again.

Then there is the story of the man, who, in the 19th century, set out to walk from Princetown to Plymouth and was accompanied for some of the way by a black dog, somewhat larger than a Newfoundland type of breed. When he tried to pat the head of the dog his hand went through it, and then, approaching Plymouth, there was a bang and a flash. The man fell into a ditch and was found next day, still unconscious. The extraordinary episode was explained by local folklore, which recalled a murder taking place at this precise place years ago. The traveller's dog haunts the stretch of road, searching for the murderer to exact revenge. In this particular case, it made a mistake.

And so the black dog stories roll along, giving entertainment and provoking much thought. Recently the tale has taken an interesting twist – a white dog apparition has been encountered in a wood on Dartmoor. Far from having flaming eyes and the personality of a revenge-crazed zombie, the white dog was gentle, and gave the impression of caring for its astounded observer.

Who knows what the next development might be?

5

The Woman Clothed
with the Sun

'– and the moon under her feet and upon her head
a crown of stars.'

This, Joanna Southcott said, very resolutely, is who she was – the woman written about in the *Book of Revelations*. And later, as if this were not enough to convince the world of her inspired spirituality, she announced that she would give birth to Shiloh, the Prince of Peace, to be created by immaculate conception.

A tall story – but Joanna Southcott became an extremely important and famous woman in the late 18th century.

She was born the daughter of a Devon farm labourer at Gittisham, near Honiton, in the spring of 1750. She attended the village school, and there began her reading of the Bible, which was probably the genesis of her beliefs and future prophecies. She did not publicly declare her mission until she was 42 years old, when she said that God had called her to a vocation of prophecy. She proclaimed that the world of violence and poverty would shortly end, and a new kingdom would be born of Shiloh – of understanding, beauty, happiness and universal love.

Such a magnificient vision spread her fame. Of course, some said she was deluded, a self-seeking opportunist, an illiterate woman deceived by the Devil. But others – and there were plenty, amounting over the years in Devon alone to 40,000 – believed Joanna wholeheartedly, and supported her ministry.

She worked at an upholsterer's shop in Exeter, and there met her Methodist employer's friends and guests, many of whom were ministers, and so sufficiently interested – even if startled – to listen to the description of her extraordinary visions and prophecies. Joanna received her visitations from God in an ecstatic state of mind, likening herself to being in the hands of a holy husband. Yet, as she grew older she began to have fears and doubts. Was it God, or was it the Devil, who put such words and images into her mind? Which was her true mentor?

After she had signed a document, in the presence of several Methodist ministers, declaring the true source of her messages to be God, it was generally accepted that her writings were to be relied upon. But Joanna was deeply wounded when the Anglican church would not support her as she had hoped. Like other Nonconformists she had to create her own sect, and so the Southcottian Society was formed.

Her flock of supporters increased until there were 100,000 members. The men grew long hair and beards, refusing to shave until the coming of Shiloh. In Exeter, children ran in fear from 'The Bearded Men' as they were called. Joanna's women support-ers were uplifted by her gentle feminism, for she told them that the time of the woman approached. One of her hymns spoke of:

> 'The woman, with the Sun array'd
> Treads down the Moon, beneath her feet.
> On her Jehovah's pow'r's displayed,
> She brings to man the light complete.'

Her writings were a mixture of strong faith and fearful doubts, but her message was surely a small and timely hope of salvation for ordinary people living in squalor and the direst poverty. Did they really believe that within a short time all wickedness and pain would depart, to be replaced by a new kingdom of love? Whether it was only the sense of hope, or a sincerely born conviction, we can never know, but Joanna's prophecies, both small personal ones, and the more universal and apocryphal, were revered and glorified. She was much loved. During her years as a visionary, she wrote several books and preached many public sermons. Membership of her Southcottian Society extended throughout

the country. When, in her later years, she announced the coming of Shiloh, her child, all England's attention was focused upon her.

By then she was 60 years old, unmarried and, one imagines, still virgin. Yet she said she was God's bride, chosen to be the mother of His son. Suddenly all the acclaim and near-adoration she had received through the long years of her ministry fell apart, crushed by the public's bawdy and coarse speculation as to her condition. Poor Joanna. Already heavily laden with confusing doubts, now she had to endure public humiliation. With experience of our own times, how well we can identify with her dismay.

No child was born, although attending doctors admitted she showed all the symptoms of pregnancy. She fell into a coma and died – on 20th December 1814 – perhaps thankfully, glad to escape further torment from a scoffing, insensitive public. Her body was kept warm for four days with hot-water bottles, in the wistful belief that she might be only entranced and not dead. One report says that she died of a brain tumour, which certainly lends support to the hint of delusion. Her funeral was kept secret, to the anger and frustration of the public press. Three people were at her graveside.

Yet Joanna's message still lives. The Ark, or Box, in which she is said to have stored her unspoken prophecies, remains intact. She had ordered that its contents should only be revealed in the presence of 24 Anglican bishops. In 1927 it was said to have been opened in the presence of the Bishop of Grantham, but there is considerable confusion as to whether the box was indeed Joanna's Ark.

Both the Southcottian Society in Sunderland, and the Panacea Society in Bedford make regular public requests for the true box to be opened in the required circumstances. Current literature published by the Panacea Society shows a drawing of the box, 'which weighs 156 lbs, is nailed with copper nails and in safe keeping.'

'Crime and Banditry, Distress and Perplexity,' says the Society, 'will increase in England until the Bishops open THIS Box.'

Strangely, the publication of a contemporary novel about Joanna Southcott's follower, John Wroe, is today making the public once again conscious of her name and beliefs. The novel has been followed by a television series, and a radio play, and so it seems that we have not yet heard the last of Joanna's strange ministry, and her box of prophecies.

But the final word in this intriguing story must be left to Ralph Whitlock, who says, in his *Folklore of Devon*, 'The Box has . . . been X-rayed and has been shown to contain a pistol and other unidentified articles.'

And so we go on waiting – for the right box to be opened, in the right circumstances. And perhaps even for 'the woman clothed with the sun' to be proved to have been, after all, a truly inspired visionary. It would be nice to believe that poor Joanna was not just a victim of religious obsession.

6

Trains that Ran on Air

The waiting passengers crowding onto Exeter station in September 1846 exchanged wry comments, full of curiosity and anticipation.

'I read in the local paper that Master Piston is becoming a general favourite . . . '

'Indeed! Also that many prefer Master Piston's noiseless approach to the long-drawn sighs of Puffing Billy!'

Laughter rippled around.

'Well, we shall see. And very soon, for here it comes . . .'

Public response to Mr Brunel's innovative atmospheric railway had been enthusiastic, hence the comments about Master Piston, the new train, and Puffing Billy, the old one – apt nicknames culled from the Devonshire press. Today the expectant passengers, having paid their appropriate fares – first class Exeter to Newton Abbot 2d, second class 1½d, and third class 1d, for a 45-minute journey – were about to see for themselves exactly what all the fuss was about. Well, here it was.

Surprise kept them motionless for a moment as the extraordinary conveyance halted beside them. The newspapers were right – no noisy, smutty locomotive! So how did the thing work?

They climbed aboard the rough, uncomfortable carriages, the guard blew his horn, a porter manipulated some sort of pipe at the front of the leading carriage, and they were off. There was a jerk, a bang, and Mr Brunel's train began its journey, stopping at the small stations all along the line and sucking in air regularly at various engine-houses.

Saucer-eyed, the passengers watched as, at Teignmouth, a proper Puffing Billy was hitched onto the piston-carriage, for the atmospheric line was not yet completed to Newton Abbot. Along the way the necessarily cold carriages were treated to an assault of hot sandbags, thrown in at each station, in an attempt to warm the passengers. And entertainment was provided, too – for among their travelling companions were the usual occasional itinerant musicians and ballad singers, who passed the time by practising their arts.

As they became used to the smooth motion of the new train, the passengers told each other that Mr Brunel's invention, already tried out in London, was just as great a success here in Devon. Such silence. Such speed. How wonderful it would be when the line reached Plymouth, as was the brilliant engineer's intention. And all without dirty locomotion – just compressed air and suction.

Isambard Kingdom Brunel's reputation as an engineer of acclaimed genius was second only to that of magnificent George Stephenson. Both men were visionaries and innovators. And this in an age when the swift development of the industrial revolution was constantly and regularly breeding other skilled engineers of talent and creativity. But Brunel – the Little Giant, as he was nicknamed, for he was a short man – had greater resolution and ambition than his contemporaries. Not only was he far-seeing, perhaps even in advance of his time, but he was also a skilled draughtsman and artist, with the unusual ability of carrying through every aspect of the work he designed. His genius, allied to his workmanship, brought him international fame during his too short lifetime. He had already planned the Great Western Railway, running from London to Exeter, and now was developing the line on to Plymouth by the means of the exciting new atmospheric power. His star was in the ascendant, and he hoped and believed that this was to be his greatest achievement. But he had his detractors: 'this atmospheric caper', they snorted indignantly.

It was certainly a strange, ingenious idea. From Exeter loco-motives were replaced by a line of linked carriages, the leading carriage sucking up exhausted air from a 15″ iron pipe laid in the centre of the broad gauge track, thus driving the train by pneumatic traction. And, despite all the early criticism of the idea, in practice these trains provided silent, clean and much smoother travel, with a maximum speed of 65–70 miles per hour.

Those first excited passengers must have had a memorable journey, as the train ran alongside the river Exe from Exeter to Teignmouth, the land clear on the far side of the gleaming estuary, small boats busy around Starcross and Exmouth harbours. Beneath a blue sky, and beside shining water, who could have asked for a better form of conveyance?

The regular doses of exhausted air which the atmospheric line required were provided by pumping stations sited at three-mile intervals along the track. There were eight in all of these tall-towered, red sandstone buildings, beginning at Exeter and ending at Newton Abbot.

Brunel was a man with an overwhelmingly charismatic personality, whose longing to realise great ambitions motivated a workaholic lifestyle. Almost aggressive in his self-confidence and determination, he was privately also prey to dark doubts. Yet he was charming, sociable and vastly entertaining, enjoying amusing his friends' children with sleight-of-hand conjuring. In the workplace he could always be found at the very heart of activity, his clothes creased and oil-stained, battered old cigar-holder hanging around his neck. He was respected, even loved, by his workmen who found him direct but honest, and always fair. In turn, the public lionised him and then dismissed him as a crank.

Mary, his wife, must have had a lonely and frustrating life, at home with their three children, always anxious about the danger to which he constantly, and thoughtlessly, exposed himself. In fact it was that very obsession with his work which brought him to an early death. While a young man he worked with his father, Marc, on the tunnel being dug beneath the river Thames in London. Here – naturally, at the very rockface – he was badly injured when the water flooded in. His kidneys were damaged, to deteriorate slowly throughout the remainder of his life. This injury, allied to a lifestyle that could never allow rest, and had little time for relaxing domesticity, finally caught up with him at the age of 53 when, weakened by chronic kidney failure, he suffered a stroke and died soon afterwards.

Such a vital man, so prodigiously successful in his various engineering achievements, was also bound to have great failures – and the atmospheric railway in Devon proved probably the greatest failure of all.

Much has been written about the doomed line which, soon after its exciting début, suffered increasingly frequent mechanical breakdowns, but the chief fault appears to have been with the valve in the iron pipe that carried the all-important air power. In order to allow entry of the piston from the carriage, the valve was made of a strip of leather, riveted to a second one. Friction occurred between iron and leather, resulting in a torn length of valve, destroying the vital vacuum.

Perhaps Brunel had overlooked one simple yet important fact – that in Devon the natural humidity of the sea air would affect the leather. Also, the lime soap used to treat the cracked leather accelerated corrosion, and so in wet weather rain filled the pipe. Mounting costs, as repairs were made, resulted in consternation and conflict within the financing company. Yes, the faults could be made good, but it would cost more than the shareholders were willing to pay.

And perhaps the last word in the failure of the atmospheric railway's short story must go to the rats which, it is said, ate the lime soap on the leather . . .

Despite initial problems, the iron pipe continued to be laid along the line to Torquay, but was never used. After a year's attempt to successfully cope with increasing breakdowns, the line was abandoned and good old Puffing Billy came back to replace poor failed Master Piston.

Isambard Brunel, his three children and Mary all loved Devon, with its fine beaches, winding lanes and misty hills. They rented a house near Torquay while he worked on the atmospheric line and he had every intention of retiring there, as his health grew weaker. He bought some land at Watcombe and even drew up plans for a house to be built. But it wasn't to be.

His final visit to Devon was in August 1859, when, weak and severely incapacitated, he lay on a couch fixed to an open carriage driven along his magnificent bridge spanning the river Tamar, to which Prince Albert had graciously given his name. Accompanied by Mary and a secretary, Brunel inspected the details of his work through a telescope. In great pain, he saw his immense and beautiful trusses arching against a vaulting blue sky, and raised a weak smile. Here, if anywhere, was a triumphant memorial to all his plans, works and dreams. He died not long after that victorious, but sad journey.

When the atmospheric railway was finally abandoned, the Teignmouth correspondent of the *Western Times* wrote a wry obituary:

> 'Farewell the tranquil mind – farewell content!
> Farewell, ye pistons, pipes, and valves, and all!
> Farewell extensive sheds, the fat grease
> That makes the valves adhesive. All farewell!
> Adieu, great air-exhausting engine-houses!
> The Atmospheric occupations gone.'

Yet not entirely gone. For beside the line along which this astonishing railway once ran is the ruined shell of one of the great pumping houses, reminding us still of Brunel's genius. Look for it beside the track at Starcross, and then visit Teignmouth museum, where a piece of the original iron pipe is on display.

7

Ladies' Amusements at A La Ronde

Having spent over ten delightful and instructive years doing the Grand Tour in Europe, Devon-born Jane Parminter and her orphaned cousin, Mary, to whom she acted as guardian, returned to England in 1795.

Jane and Mary, both spinsters, brought back with them an enormous amount of souvenirs, enough to fill even the most accommodating cabinet of curiosities, so prized in those days. But perhaps even more important than the evocative treasures were the vivid memories of foreign lands visited, together with new ideas of reforming the social structure of the age in which they lived. Impressions of varied cultures and religions resulted in Jane planning an extremely unusual house, based upon the church of San Vitale, which she and Mary had visited in Ravenna. As she set about finding a site for their new home, Jane's resolution and slightly eccentric character also set in motion a mode of life and good works that was to survive the next two centuries and intrigue many thousands of people.

Her married sister, Marianne, had already settled in Exmouth, a newly-fashionable seaside resort with a long, sandy beach, so perhaps it was Marianne's fond persuasion that caused Jane to buy 15 acres of land just outside the village. She certainly had an eye for beauty, for the high spot of land she chose looked down on a delectable landscape, stretching from the Haldon Hills in the east to beyond Exmouth's furthest red sandstone rocks in the west.

The house that was built among the lush fields, bordered by massive oak trees – which were to become part of the continuing

Parminter story – was, by the standards of those Regency times, an extraordinary and unconventional one.

'A curious looking modern building,' commented a visitor in 1866. 'Something between a house and a Temple of a circular shape and with a fantastic Chinese looking ornamental roof.' What must have the simple Exmouth folk thought, as they gaped at the ornate building arising on the hill?

Despite its name – A La Ronde – the house was not circular but octagonal, with interconnecting rooms, each with a small wedge-shaped lobby at its side that completed and linked the unusual shape. The Misses Parminter's purpose in designing their home with such singular originality was to enable them to follow the circuit of the sun each day, always having a light room in which to sit – no doubt a legacy of their past years spent in warmer places.

The central hall was the hub of the house, with stairs leading to a gallery some 35 ft from the ground floor. If the intricate design of the rooms was not already proof of Jane's artistic planning, then the grotto-style gallery settled the issue without further question. For here the cousins lavished time and immense creativity in covering every inch of the stairs, walls and ceilings with shell-work of great beauty and imaginative power.

Jane's early life in Lisbon, where her father had business interests, combined with her years of travel throughout France, Germany, Italy, Switzerland and Spain to influence her work at A La Ronde. She and Mary must have filled long days collecting shells from Exmouth beach, or sending away elsewhere for additional stocks. And not just shells, for seaweed and bird feathers, grasses, mica, straw, lichen, pottery, stones, bones and sand were all used as media for the decorative patterns. Up and down stepladders they must have gone daily, practising their Regency 'ladies' amusements', for surely no artists of their calibre were content with watching a servant clumsily mis-carrying out their beautiful schemes?

Other rooms besides the gallery received the ladies' precise ministrations – seaweed pictures, shell collections of many designs and feather friezes, with each gamebird feather put on card before being stuck into its appropriate place in the pattern,

appeared all over the interior of the little house. Cut paper-work was another craft they practised with tiny, sharp scissors, and they added their own cut-out images, black against white, their profiles and capped heads demure and elegant, to the other decorations filling the house.

A wonderful silhouette of the young Parminter family, drawn in 1783, hangs over the fireplace in the drawing room, painted in Indian ink by a French artist. Jane is watering her plants, while her family carry out individual pleasurable pursuits. John Parminter, her brother, stands near Marianne, who is playing the fortepiano. Elizabeth, her other sister, is making lace. Her brother-in-law, Mr Frend, is reading.

One imagines that the hooped skirts and high-dressed hair styles in the silhouette had been changed for simpler fashions by the time Jane and Mary settled in Exmouth, for if the rooms of A La Ronde are minuscule, the staircases and passages are even more so. Carrying candlesticks and oil lamps around the house at night, or on winter days when no sun shone, must have been a hazardous operation enough, without the added dangers of those earlier fashionable, but inconvenient, toilettes.

We are told that the two Parminter ladies became reclusive as well as eccentric, but this is hard to believe. Surely they invited friends to come and admire their prestigious 'amusements'? And the fortepiano itself, still to be seen, suggests musical evenings, with Jane or Mary – maybe both – obliging with an air of the day. Melodious duets perhaps filled the room, with one of the gentlemen kindly holding a candlestick. Oil lamps glowed, and candles flickered during those happy evenings, and, looking up into the dark lantern of the gallery, they might well have seen a sudden iridescent gleam of a moving flame reflecting against mother of pearl, or abalone, high above.

Surrounding the house were pleasure gardens, full of inspired planting and ornaments – surely another hint of conviviality. And the huge oaks in the surrounding fields provided a discreet screen, so that the Parminters and their friends could enjoy their privacy, sitting in the sun, appreciating the incomparable view, and exchanging opinions as they endeavoured to put the world to rights.

It was this last facet of both women's thinking that became the continuing motivation of their lives, for from it was born a shared 'point-in-view', a cryptic abstraction which manifested itself in the later building of a small chapel, school and almshouses, not far from A La Ronde.

No doubt the experiences of the cosmopolitan Grand Tour had influenced both women, and it was also a time of strong urgings for reform, both to social structures and in Noncomformist religions. The Parminter 'point-in-view' was the fervent belief in the conversion of Jews to Christianity, prior to their promised return to Palestine, and both women pursued this ideal with all the enthusiasm and resolution already evident in the designing and decorating of their home.

Because the ladies found their weekly journey into Exmouth on Sundays cold and even dangerous in winter – no macadamised roads, and only unpredictable horsepower to convey them – they decided to build their own little place of worship close enough to the house to be able to reach it safely on foot. In 1811 the 'Point-in-view,' chapel was built. Inscribed on the entrance door was the sentence 'Some Points-in-View we all Pursue', which has intrigued visitors ever since. The Parminters' religious point is clearly understood, and the view from the chapel extends to include that continuation of the sandbar, known in Exmouth as The Point – did it also suggest that worshippers should try and discover their own particular points-in-view?

Whatever the precise meaning, the chapel's outstanding feature was 'the Point' – the small tower with latticed windows and the weathervane in the semblance of a pigeon of peace, a symbolic reminder of the Parminters' Huguenot origins. In recent years it has been discovered that the whole building of the tiny chapel was covered on the outside in the same shell-work as the ladies had used so bizarrely inside their house. This has only come to light since early documents were found among the Trustees' minutes, giving assent to the removal of the weather-worn and spoilt shell covering. What a sight Point-in-View must have been on a bright sunlit day, with every side of it reflecting the light and gleaming out, like a beacon, across the countryside.

The chapel is certainly unique. Under its small roof were crammed five rooms – the Point Room itself, directly beneath the tower where worship took place before a congregation of twenty-five, a minister's residence of one room, and three other small rooms which were almshouses. It was necessary to acquire a Certificate of Dispensation to practise Nonconformist worship in the chapel, and this was given by the Bishop of Exeter.

Soon after the opening of the Point-in-View chapel, Jane Parminter died. She was buried in the vault beneath the sanctuary, but Mary continued the good work her cousin had started. Eighteen months after Jane's death, a Trust deed was drawn up, entitled 'Mary

Parminter's Charity, or the Point-in-View at A La Ronde, near Exmouth.' The details of the Trust – to which Mary contributed substantial funds – demanded that a Protestant Dissenting minister should live and teach within the chapel, that the almshouses should provide homes for four single, elderly spinsters, and that one of the inhabitants should act as schoolmistress, teaching reading and plain work to six poor, female children. It also ordered that, in the case of a Jewess who had embraced Christianity, she should be chosen rather than others. The six children were also preferred to be of Jewish parents.

It appears that little is known about the first few years of the chapel's existence, save that no minister was appointed and no doubt local preachers gave their services to the small congregation. Mary's funds were quickly swallowed; dutifully she gave more, and there is a belief that a London barrister, chancing upon A La Ronde and becoming interested, also helped in the chapel's growth.

During recent years, since the discovery of the minutes of the Trustees' meetings dating from 1822, more information has come to light. Quite naturally, the original requirements of the Trust have been modified. It is thought that no converted Jewesses ever lived in the almshouses, and that no children in the school were of Jewish parentage. But the school room was certainly used. Today one can see an original bench desk beneath the window, and an oak pull-up desk above it. It's easy to imagine small children sitting there, obediently stumbling through Bunyan's *Pilgrim's Progress*, and stitching at their samplers and household sewing. Each child was given a green stuff gown, a straw bonnet trimmed with pale green ribbon, a linen cap and a handsome Vandyke tippet.

During services in the Point Room, worshippers were encouraged to donate alms in the two small wooden collecting boxes, still in position. One is for the good of the Jews and the other for the benefit of the pastor. A minute of the Trustees' records how these boxes were solemnly emptied at the end of meetings, and how, once, the Jews received largesse of 1s 9½d to the pastor's meagre 5½d.

Mary Parminter lived a long and excellent life, and had the satisfaction of seeing the chapel she and her cousin had created become well known and widely used. In 1829 a manse was built behind it in order to house the minister, who was previously fitted into the inadequate entrance room. Over the years alterations in seating enabled the capacity of the chapel to grow, and in 1878 a pipe organ was given as a gift, handmade by the incumbent of the day.

Mary Parminter died on Tuesday, 18th December 1849, after an illness of ten or twelve days. She was eighty-two and respected for her 'intelligence, generosity, simplicity and uprightness', to quote from the minutes of a special meeting of the Trustees on 27th December. Her burial was a solemn affair. 'The Point-in-View Sepulchre having gathered to itself the last of the two excellent ladies for whom it had been prepared, and the Coffins being deposited in an Oak-Chest on the floor of the Sepulchre Chamber, it was Resolved, that to prevent the disturbance of the dead, or the inconvenience to the living, the said Oak-Chest be enclosed in a nine-inch brickwall arched over and effectually cemented . . . '

Today, in the Sanctuary, the Misses Parminter's marble memorial has pride of place, their names inscribed within a swirl of acanthus – or could it be their favourite seaweed? The famous oak trees, which the ladies ordered must never be felled until the Jews return to Israel, when their timber should be used to build the necessary ships, still stand, watchful and sheltering.

By 1971 modernisations had been carried out to the benefit of the ladies in the cramped almshouses, and three new bungalows were built beside the manse. In 1978 two more were added, with the provision that a retired minister and his wife should be housed there. The manse has a unique window in the shape of a latticed diamond, reflecting the design of A La Ronde, not far away.

The chapel now has a loved and serene atmosphere, which also encloses the manse and its neighbouring bungalows. Small gardens are immaculately tended and the happy little community – hand-chosen because of individual needs – lives at peace. Marriages in the Point Chapel are becoming popular, with subsequent growth in congregation. The Charity is administered by eight dedicated Trustees and the chapel remains open every day until dusk, affording a small oasis of peace in a busy and harrassed world.

A La Ronde is cared for by the National Trust, and is open from May to October. The famous Parminter silhouette is on view in the drawing room, but the fortepiano stands silent, maybe remembering the tunes once played upon it. Tiny, sharp-scissors used for cut paper-work, and the little machine on which Elizabeth made her lace, are all intact and on view. The shell gallery is currently being restored and not open to the public, but a video can be seen, giving details of the Parminters' fabulous craftsmanship as they practised their 'ladies' amusements'.

Great relief is naturally felt that this ancient and out-of-the-ordinary house is now in safe hands, its future secure. But what of the Point-in-View chapel? At present the Trustees perform a difficult task with excellent results, but there is no guarantee, as there is with the house, that funds and care will always appear. Yet such a unique and beautiful place as the chapel also deserves a safe future.

One can only hope that this particular 'ladies' amusement' – the Parminters' personal Point-in-View – will weather the uncertainty of the years to come.

8

Church Surprises

Nothing surprising to be found in old churches, you think? You'd be surprised!

St Brannoc's church spire, at Braunton in North Devon, was used in the past as a landmark for passing mariners. The ruins of Charles church, set within a roundabout in Plymouth, where roads enter the city from Exeter, Tavistock and Kingsbridge, have been left as a reminder of man's inhumanity to man – a memorial to the civilians killed in Plymouth in the blitz of 1941 in Hitler's war.

Ancient horseshoes decorating the little church of St Blaise at Haccombe, near Newton Abbot, are the relics of a half-forgotten story of a Champernowne lordling from Dartington challenging a Carew from Haccombe to a contest. Which man could swim his horse furthest out to sea? Neither won, for the current proved stronger than either of them, and it was one of the gallant horses, rescuing both men, that achieved fame in the shape of having its shoes nailed for posterity on the thick oak door of the church.

These are only a few of the unexpected snippets of history and folk memory that can be discovered when visiting Devon's churches. Such tales add enormous human interest to buildings that were originally erected in praise of abstract ideas.

Our Celtic ancestors created their temples in oak groves and on high hills, revering and sacrificing to the gods of nature. When the Saxons came they built small wooden churches for the glorification of their own pantheon of gods. Christianity had the wisdom and tact to allow these old sacred sites to remain in situ, but with a new dedication to Christian saints. And out of this thickly woven tapestry of mixed beliefs has grown a vast mantle of recorded fact, myth and folklore. It contains many surprises indeed, and more than a few are well worth the telling.

Barrel roofs, elaborately, if crudely, carved roof bosses, wooden rood-screens fashioned by master craftsmen – all are mute reminders of past lives. Memorial brasses on walls and floors, monuments and marble effigies of long-dead local families, all have their own stories to relate. Usually, church histories will include some interesting facts about the men and women who, over the generations, have worshipped there. Sometimes benefactors left charities for the poor of the parish. Windows have been erected to the memory of the famous, the brave and the aristocratic. Old bells in four-square granite towers have individual voices and are engraved with the names of their casters. Finely embroidered footstools are now to be seen in most churches, continuing a tradition of worship by toiling hands. Look about you, and make connections. Above all, look upwards.

It is often in the church roof that you will find the oldest bit of the ongoing story. Indistinct faces may stare down at you out of the past. Kings' and queens' heads, coats of arms, angels, symbols of things long forgotten, the image of a stonemason's pet cat – and even reminders of the paganism which first created this sacred site.

Look particularly for the green man. He is a ferocious carved effigy – a head, with foliage sprouting from ears, eyes, mouth and nostrils, an emblem of the erupting life force, the first deity to exist. Somehow the green man has slipped past the watchful eyes of Christian restorers in nearly 60 Devon churches. He can be found in 16 alone in Exeter – even the awe-inspiring Norman cathedral has a green man boss high up in the roof.

Other pagan symbols have been allowed to remain on the caps of church pillars, on bench ends and around fonts. At Luppitt church, near Honiton, the spectacular Norman font – found in the churchyard hedge during the last century – is covered with deep, primitive carvings, on which the symbolism of the Wild Hunt conveys ancient worship of Odin, the hunter, who drove across the night sky at the time of the winter solstice, carrying the souls of the dead on his wild horses' backs.

Sometimes, inside a church, you may find an ancient oak chest, once used as the Parish Chest, an important security long before safes were invented. Here were kept the Parish Registers and other documents. Now, if they have survived the centuries, they may be used for other purposes. At Sampford Courtenay church, the chest was originally hollowed out from a solid block of oak. It stands, in great and ancient dignity, on its own, and is said to have been used for the altar table of the first Protestant service in the 16th century.

Parish Registers, kept nowadays in Public Record Offices, are precious records of past local lives. The register for Uffculme records a grim time in village history, when plague – the Great Mortality, as it was first known, only later becoming the Black Death – swept all before it. We are told that there were '38 burials in one year, 27 taking place in the first 14 days of August.' Many other Devon villages were similarly affected, and the population of England itself is said to have been reduced by as much as a third through this virulent epidemic.

But the story of sweet Humphy Degon of Ilsington, is a far happier example of times past . . .

Sweet Humphy Degon

Tuesday morning the 17th of September 1639 was wet. Not all the boy scholars who usually attended Master Hanniball Corbyn's school in the little room above the lychgate of St Michael's church had presented themselves. But Humphy was there. Somehow his family had found the few pennies necessary to give him some basic education. Humphy was learning to read the Good Book and to sign his name, in the hope that he would do more with his life than spend it tilling fields, a hard and disrupting existence, of constant physical labour and relentless poverty.

Master Corbyn, a part-time schoolmaster, who was a tailor by trade and himself trying to improve his lot, was a disciplinarian, and the boys who laboured in the crowded little room had their minds keenly concentrated on three things that fateful September morning: trying to remember what they'd been taught yesterday, endeavouring to write scrawling pothooks, and – most important of all – keeping

44

one eye open for Master Corbyn's ever-present stick.

Like the remainder of the church, the lychgate was extremely old. Beneath its curving timbers and bulging plaster the gate swung heavily, creaking its resentment at being used so thoughtlessly by those passing through.

Nearly eleven o'clock. Small stomachs rumbled and Master Corbyn laid down his cane, just about to announce that it was dinner time. But before the boys could make the usual mad dash for the door – it happened.

A woman pushed shut the gate, which, at the end of its tether, finally rebelled. Hinges split, rocks moved, timbers splintered, and the porch collapsed. Four boys fell into the churchyard. One ran into the chimney of the schoolroom and escaped harm. Falling beams and crashing masonry took other boys with them as they fell, like a torrent. And sweet Humphy, aged six, fell amid the masonry of the east wall into the street, where he lay buried and invisible.

The noise brought villagers from their homes and fields. Bare hands dug into the rubble. Men raced around, finding spades and picks – anything at all to get out the victims, surely dead or dying beneath that swirling dust.

Amazingly, all the boys were found to be safe, unhurt but for a few sore heads and aching limbs. Mothers hugged their filthy sons and hustled them off home. But Humphy stayed where he was, a small, battered body, trapped by boulders and rotting timbers. It was some time before his mother was alerted and went looking for him.

She found Master Corbyn, bruised and dusty, but unhurt, searching, too. Together they fearfully pulled away the debris, staring down at the boy's begrimed body.

'My sweet Humphy . . . '

Mistress Degon pulled the child up into her arms. Then, disbelieving, she and Master Corbyn watched Humphy's eyes slowly open wide. Not dead. Not even hurt.

There were celebrations that day in Ilsington, and prayers were offered up in church. 'to the everlasting praise of God, in memory of wonderful deliverance.'

Today we can look at the rebuilt lychgate and marvel again at the deliverance Master Hanniball Corbyn recorded so meticulously, in the church register, some three and a half centuries ago.

Another poignant life story is remembered in North Devon. In Heanton Punchardon churchyard look for a headstone with a handbell set in the stone, above a few lines of engraved verse.

Edward Capern, the Postman Poet, lies here, long forgotten now, after an early life of rural poverty which ended in national fame and a ceremonial funeral, with his coffin draped in the Union Jack.

Born to poor parents in Tiverton in 1819, Edward worked, as a boy of eight, in the local lace factory. The close work strained his eyes, but of greater concern to him than failing sight was to teach himself to read and write. In 1847 he became a letter carrier, walking 13 miles a day from Bideford to Buckland Brewer, seven days a week, for ten shillings and sixpence. It must have been a struggle, supporting a wife and family on that small wage, but Edward was apparently a genial and optimistic man, and nothing could stop the poems and songs – and flute music – that poured out of him.

His poems were written in praise of the beauty of the scenery of his native North Devon, and such was their appeal that, in 1856, a Barnstaple benefactor organised a local subscription list which financed the publication of Edward's first book of poems.

Success followed. His wages were raised to 13 shillings a week, and he was excused Sunday duties. After a poem, entitled The Lion Flag of England, was circulated as a broadsheet among troops fighting in the Crimea, the prime minister of the day awarded him a Civil List Pension of £40 a year and, following the second and third editions of his poems, he became a national celebrity. A success story is always warming to hear, and one feels this couldn't have happened to a nicer and more deserving man.

Edward Capern continued writing until his death in 1894. Sadly, his poems are forgotten now, but the few lines engraved on his headstone – below that evocative and well-used handbell – were written by the Poet Laureate, Alfred Austin, and can give us some idea of the esteem in which the Postman Poet was held in late Victorian days.

> 'O lark like poet! Carol on
> Lost in dim light and unseen till
> We in the heaven where you are gone
> Find you no more but hear you still.'

Outside Devon churches, God's little acres vary from huge to small, from neatly mown to all-but-forgotten. Yet churchyards, with their tilting, lichened, often tumbledown gravestones, can teach us much of the varying spans of life allotted to humans through the past seven or eight centuries.

Read some of the lovely old Devon names – Hannah, Josia, Walter, Joshua and Charlotte – and decipher a few moss-covered epitaphs, and I guarantee that not only will you be entertained, but sometimes deeply moved, for here are recorded the vagaries of life, with all its pitfalls, tragedies and occasional happinesses – and even a smattering of home-spun philosophy, which still makes sense today.

At Kingsbridge, in the south of Devon, is the epitaph of Bone Phillips, an 18th-century barrel-maker, who drank deeply. He must have been quite a character.

> 'Here lie I at the Chancel Door,
> Here lie I because I'm poor.
> The further in the more you'll pay.
> Here lie I as warm as they.'

And then, at Meavy, on the southern side of Dartmoor, are words bringing back to life the village blacksmith who died, aged 80, in 1827:

> 'My Sledge and my hammer both decline
> My bellows too have lost their wind
> My fire's extinguished, my forge decayed,
> And, in the dust, my vice is laid.
> My coal is spent, my iron's gone.
> My nails are drove, my work is done.'

Robert Herrick, the 17th-century minister at Dean Prior church, said unkind things about Devon, and as he was thrown out of his vicarage by Cromwell, he muttered, 'Dean Bourn farewell: I never look to see Dean, or thy warty incivility.' But this is the same man who wrote moving words about his maid, Prue, who, like him, lies in an unnamed grave in Dean Prior churchyard. He wrote of her, in 1640:

'In this little urn is laid,
Prudence Baldwin (once my maid)
From whose happy spark here let
Spring the purple violet.'

In Dartmouth, the epitaph of Tom Goldsmith demands attention:

'THOMAS GOLDSMITH. Commander of the Snap-Dragon, a privateer, in the reign of Queen Anne, in which vessel he turned pirate and amassed much riches.

Men that are virtuous fear the Lord,
And the devil's by his friends adored;
And as they merit, get a place
Amidst the blest, or hellish race;
Pray then, ye learned clergy, show
Where can this brute, Tom Goldsmith, go;
Whose life was one continued evil,
Striving to cheat God, man, and devil.'

A notable lady is commemorated in Barnstaple church. Her epitaph is a tribute to an actress:

'Underneath the Library of this Church Resteth
Until the Archangel's Trump
Shall summon her to appear on an immortal stage,
The body of Elizabeth Burton, Comedian,
Formerly of Drury Lane, but late of the Exeter Theatre;
Who exchanged time for eternity on All-Soul's Day, 1771,
Aged 20 years.

Life's but a walking shadow; A poor player,
Who struts his hour or two upon the stage;
And then is heard no more.
This small tribute To the memory of An amiable young woman,
An innocent, cheerful companion, And most excellent actress,
Was placed here by J.Foote, Manager of the Theatre.'

Another praiseworthy soul, who is remembered not only for her devotion to duty but for the sting in the tail of her epitaph, was Ann Clark, midwife of Tiverton, who died in 1733, aged 77. Between 1698 and 1733 she delivered over 5,000 children.

'On harmless babes I did attend,
Whilst I on earth my life did spend;
To help the helpless in their need,
I ready was with care and speed.
Many from pain my hands did free,
But none from death could rescue me:
My glass is run, my hour is past,
And yours is coming all too fast.'

Devoted and knowledgeable as she undoubtedly was, even Ann Clark would have been unable to stop the death toll of the smallpox epidemic of later years. In Walkhampton churchyard these sad words haunt the memory:

'Here lies 3 children of Benjamin and Anne Dunstone
Richard died November 3rd 1769 aged 10 months
George died November 5th 1769 aged 8 years
Anthony died November 7th 1769 aged 4 years.
Our tender bodies the smallpox would not spare
That mortal sickness was too severe
Unto our bodies but our souls do reign
In heaven with Christ without spot or stain.'

But a memorable epitaph in St Michael's church at Torrington, in North Devon, does much to balance the pain and grief that life inevitably inflicts. What a happy marriage this must have been . . .

'She was, but words are wanting to say what.
Think what a wife should be and she was that.'

Yet, possibly, not quite so realistic as this:

'Here lies the body of Mary Sexton,
Who pleas'd many a man, but never vex'd one;
Not like the woman who lies under the next stone.'

9

Dartmoor Letterboxes

When James Perrott, owner of a fishing-tackle shop in Chagford in 1854, established himself as a 'Tourists' Guide to Dartmoor', he set in motion a ball which is today rolling faster and with more diversifications than he could ever have imagined. A guide for over 50 years, it was he who started the fashion for discovering letterboxes hidden on the moor.

The first letterbox, if it can so be called, for it was simply a glass jar set inside a newly built stone cairn, was established at Cranmere Pool. Both romantically and physically Cranmere has always been considered the 'heart of the moor', and thus the spot every committed walker wanted to visit.

In 1856 Murray's *Handbook for Travellers* in Devon and Cornwall reported that 'the miraculous pool was never above 220 yards in circumference and is now partially, if not entirely, drained by the removal of peat from its banks. It is invested with a certain mystery which has probably arisen from its isolation in the midst of such desolate bogs and from the many fruitless attempts made by travellers to discover it.'

And so James Perrott, with admirable astuteness, took the opportunity that popular fancy offered, and led his visitors through hazardous ups and downs, around mires and bogs, and over miles of wet tussocks which necessitated much energetic bog-hopping. The shortest route was 7½ miles – each way – but ladies were taken along a slightly easier path of 9 miles – again, each way – because of the inconvenience of their unsuitable Victorian clothing.

Did they appreciate the pool when they got there? Perhaps not completely, for by the time James Perrott's business was thriving, Cranmere Pool had become a small depression in a bleak peat bog, hardly the romantic spot conjured up by legend and anticipation. But the fact of finding a letterbox there was something of a carrot – visitors left their cards in the glass jar, thus publicising their valour in having achieved the difficult journey. By 1889 a tin box had been substituted for the jar, so numerous were the cards left there.

In April 1905, two dedicated walkers put a visitors' book in the tin with the request that names and impressions should be left in the book, adding 'postcards or letters left in the box will be posted by the next caller, who will please write on them the date at which he takes them away.' Within the next three years 1,741 signatures had been collected, and the visitors' books were regularly renewed. These are now stored in Plymouth Library.

The fashion for visiting letterboxes grew, with variations. In 1894 a 'time capsule' containing some coins and newspaper cuttings, together with the usual visitors' book, was hidden somewhere on the north moor, close to Belstone Tor. Its exact situation was a secret – it could have been either at Taw Marsh or Belstone – and this was kept until the early 1940s, each finder respecting the secrecy and not divulging the site. In 1940, however, the Water Board planned works in the vicinity of the tor, and so action was taken. Now there is a letterbox at both of these sites, and the secret is public knowledge.

But another famous letterbox had already been placed at Duck's Pool, in the centre of the southern moor, in 1938. This was to commemorate William Crossing, the great walker and chronicler of Dartmoor. Here the box was made of teak with a zinc lining and contained the usual visitors' book, a stamp pad and a rubber stamp. A bronze tablet was fixed to a large granite boulder close by, and engraved, 'In memory of William Crossing, author of many inspiring books on Dartmoor, whose Guide is a source of invaluable information to all lovers of the moor. Died 3rd September 1928 aged 80'. Duck's Pool letterbox has been renewed over the years and is thought now to be quite as popular as that at Cranmere Pool.

Now the scene was set for more and more letterboxes to be hidden and searched for. In 1951 Fur Tor was favoured, Crow Tor came next in 1962, and others followed – Hen Tor, Grant's Pot (an underground cavern) and Grim's Grave.

In all, by 1964, seven letterboxes were established. And then in 1977 there was an explosion of them and numerous caches were suddenly put in place all over Dartmoor. The object was to allow searchers to collect impressions of the rubber stamp each box contained, as well as signing the visitors' books in the usual way.

Thus was born the continuing contemporary passion for 'letter-boxing', a 'sport for all seasons' as it has been aptly termed. Today it is rare if, walking the moor, one does not meet groups of keen letterboxers searching for the next elusive box and its prized stamp.

Letterboxes have also been set up inside several moorland pubs. Initially, this was to enable handicapped searchers to reach their goals more easily, but the inns concerned quickly became established venues for letterboxers. Chat and information is exchanged and camaraderie – an essential part of the sport – grows. The Plume of Feathers at Princetown, the Forest Inn at Hexworthy, the Ring O'Bells at North Bovey, the Tavistock Inn at Poundsgate, the Ten Tors at Kingsteignton and, of course, the internationally famous Warren House Inn, standing high on the lonely road running from Moretonhampstead to Princetown and beyond, are the chosen venues.

The 100 Club is an exclusive and unusual gathering of letter-boxers – a club that has 'no committee, no club premises and is not really existing', to quote Anne Swinscow, a prime mover in the popular sport, and author of several books on the subject. 'The only requirement for membership is that one must have visited 100 different Dartmoor Letterboxes.' The reward is a small cloth badge, which achieving members wear proudly on future sorties over the moor.

Letterboxing for charity has been another offshoot of the movement and much good work has been done here. But the following of this popular hobby, which gives interest and enjoyment to countless people, including families with children of all ages, has stirred up conflict within the boundaries of the moor.

At one point, the Dartmoor National Park Authority issued warnings about landowners' walls and buildings, and antiquities, being damaged in the fervent search for the hidden box. This was, however, resolved by mutual agreement, and now a strict code of conduct exists which warns of the danger, also forbidding the placing of letterboxes in any potentially dangerous situation, and finally making it clear that cement or other building material should not be used to make a fixture.

Occasionally individual landowners on the moor have grown restive at the sight of searchers toppling their enclosure walls, and so have personally removed any boxes found on their property. But on the whole letterboxers continue to happily seek out fresh caches and hide new boxes, and the diversifications have developed into the inclusion of topical poems in visitors' books.

Many verses are in 'sing-song chant', in couplets and in pure doggerel, but there are also some in imitation of more epic works. How will future antiquarians and archaeologists, researching the moor in centuries to come, react to some of these letterboxing masterpieces?

Here is a flavour of the local talent – to be sung to the tune of a favourite harvest hymn:

'We scour the Moor for boxes
Well scattered o'er the land,
Just put there for our pleasure
By someone else's hand.
We brave the snow in Winter,
To cross the rough terrain,
We climb the tors in Summer,
Through driving sleet and rain.
(John Hayward)

Among the plethora of verses now proliferating on the moor, there are some amusing and clever reworkings of many moorland legends. But without doubt this short couplet, also by author John Hayward, aptly sums up the whole business of letterboxing on Dartmoor:

'Rubber stamps in letter boxes
Aching feet, and soggy soxes.'

54

10

Mysterious Chambercombe

In 1865 farmer Jan Vyles was repairing the roof of his home in Ilfracombe when he discovered a small, blocked-up window beneath the edge of the thatch.

In the past it was quite common to find such windows, for the introduction of the Window Tax in 1696 had resulted in many householders cannily bricking up the taxable commodities. But the strange thing about this particular window at Chambercombe Manor was that Jan knew there was no corresponding room inside his old house. Intrigued, he inspected the bedrooms very carefully. Yes, each room and each window was accounted for. Clearly then, the only way to solve the mystery was to take a pickaxe to the nearest wall . . .

With the wall broken down, Jan wished he hadn't been so curious, for what met his astonished gaze was very unpleasant. He saw a shadowy, secret room ahead of him, shrouded with cobwebs and the dust of centuries.

Though small, it was a fully furnished room with a chair and a table, mouldering tapestries hanging on the walls – and a four-poster bed, swathed in curtains. He shouted for a candle to be brought, then cautiously approached the bed. As he touched the fragments of heavy curtain they disintegrated and, shocked, he looked down upon a skeleton, sparsely covered with tattered remains of old-fashioned clothing.

In due course Jan arranged for the bones to be buried. The skeleton was found to be that of a young woman and was given a pauper's grave in Ilfracombe churchyard. No doubt Jan became a seven-day celebrity, and folklore started weaving its irrepressible threads, using the few known facts, and then, in the time-honoured fashion, supposing this, imagining that. Finally, two versions of the mysterious story came into being.

The skeleton on the bed – according to the first version – was that of Kate Oatway, and had been lying there for the past 150 years until Jan broke down the wall. Kate was the daughter of a notorious wrecker and smuggler, William, who lived at Chambercombe Manor in the 17th century. The tunnel that linked the house with Hele beach was known to have been used in his criminal activities. Kate, married to Tristan Wallace, an officer in the Irish Army, was making a visit home to her parents in Ilfracombe when her ship was lured onto the rocks by wreckers – none other than her father and his cronies. These savage men allowed no survivors as witnesses of their hideous practices, and so all crew and passengers were either drowned or killed on that fateful night, Kate among them. Her father, at last discovering what he had done, carried her body home through the tunnel and up to the little room, where she was laid on the four-poster bed. Then he walled up the room.

No one knows what happened to William Oatway after that terrible night. Did he repent and live out the remainder of his life trying, in vain, to make amends for past crimes? Did he perhaps move away, unable to stay in the house with the rotting body of his daughter beneath the same roof?

Folklore stops short at this point, save to add that once Kate's bones were disturbed, her ghost began haunting the house. She has been seen walking the passages, passing through the bedrooms and in the cobbled courtyard outside the building.

But – interrupts the second version of the tale – what if Kate had actually been someone quite different? The wife, perhaps, of William Oatway, who discovered her husband's smuggling secrets and had to be silenced, as she threatened to tell the authorities? Or even someone quite unconnected with the Oatway family? A rich, titled lady who escaped the wreckers, only to be taken alive as the smugglers claimed their booty, and carried to Chambercombe where she was abused, robbed of her jewels and money and then bricked up . . .

And there is yet another voice to be heard in the complex web of intrigue, this one insisting that the ghost who haunts Chambercombe is that of Lady Jane Grey, Queen for nine days, before being beheaded in 1554. The Earl of Suffolk, Lord Grey, was an early owner of Chambercombe. His plastered coat of arms decorates the wall over the fireplace in the Elizabethan bedroom. It is known that young Jane toured the area, visiting her Devonshire relations, before she was manipulated onto England's throne.

Perhaps, for some reason, her spirit returns to the old house.

So the various tales are told, but still Chambercombe retains its mysterious secrets.

Today, visitors to this fascinating and atmospheric ancient house, once a Domesday manor, enlarged and beautified in Tudor times, are regaled with yet more fresh and colourful stitches in the tapestry of local folklore. Footsteps have been heard climbing stairs that are no longer there. The steps are so loud and heavy that their owner must surely be carrying something – no doubt it is the ghost of William Oatway, bringing his daughter's body upstairs before hiding her away in the secret room, so soon to be hidden from the world's gaze.

The dark little room is unfurnished now and is an evocative and mute memory of past events. It jolts the visitor out of complacency – after peering into the shadows and imagining what happened here long ago it is only too easy to accept the continuation of the legend. For now a poltergeist has joined the spirit of Kate – or is she Jane? – who prowls the house at night. A particular candlestick cannot be left in the Elizabethan bedroom with other candlesticks because something, or someone, comes in and throws it to the floor.

Now it stands – and remains untouched – on the windowsill of the first bedroom, facing visitors as they enter, and reminding them that this is a house where extraordinary things happened in the past – and are still happening today.

11

George Templer and the Haytor Granite Tramway

The 16th September 1820 saw a festive scene at Haytor, on Dartmoor, long to be remembered. It was the triumphal opening of George Templer's granite tramway – an innovative method of transporting quarried granite from the moor to the port of Teignmouth.

Farmers and labourers from neighbouring villages climbed the grassy slopes of Haytor Down that morning, some begging lifts from passing wagons and carts. Horses wore ceremonial brasses, and even the poorest labourer's wife had found a precious bit of bright ribbon to signify the importance of the event. And in the quarrymen's mind was the vital thought – if this mad new idea of wagons, laden with dressed granite blocks, pulled by teams of horses and travelling down the rough hillside on tracks made of that same granite, really works, then surely the improved speed of delivery must mean better times for us all?

So they cheered George Templer and his lovely, sweet-voiced wife when they appeared, surrounded by a group of the county's aristocrats. A brace of lords and at least three baronets and their ladies, all wearing elegant clothes such as poor labouring families had never dreamed of. Flimsy muslins, fanciful bonnets – fine-bred horseflesh, magnificent carriages – and voices that common folk could scarcely understand.

But ale and cider soon mellowed the picnickers, and by the time George Templer made his speech about his dream for new days and new ways, they were captivated. His voice wafted into the air above them, silencing even the praises of the trilling skylarks, his charm and enthusiasm entrancing the audience even further. When finally, *God Save The King* bellowed forth, the man who had created this strange new stone tramway seemed almost a god to the simple minds gathered there on the Haytor slopes.

George Templer's father, James, had also been an innovator, but within a different medium. He had made a canal at Ventiford, near his home at Stover, just outside Newton Abbot, to carry the china clay his company dug from the Bovey Basin. Barges travelled through five locks to the river Teign, from where they were poled and sailed down to Teignmouth, and then on up-country. James had left a fortune, and a standard of integrity and commitment to business which George found hard to emulate.

For, although the granite tramway proved successful, George was not the man his father had been. Certainly he did his best. The creation of the tramway had been a spark of necessary creative thinking when faced with a contract to supply granite for the rebuilding of London Bridge. And George also built a new quay at Teignmouth to expand his business opportunites. With the tramway gently easing the great loads of dressed stone down the hillside from the quarries, and then the empty carts being pulled uphill again by teams of horses, the Haytor granite business must have seemed set fair for the future.

Yet, some eight years later, George Templer was obliged to sell up – and not only the tramway and the canal, but also his beloved Stover estate. The catastrophe was caused by many things, as such disasters always are. One factor was possibly the inefficient work of the men whom he had placed in high positions within his company. But chiefly it seems to have been George Templer's own expensive and indulgent lifestyle that forced the sale.

Charming and handsome, a true friend, with a ready wit, well-educated and with a penchant for writing attractive verse, there is no doubt about George Templer's magnetic and likeable personality. Stover was always full of guests. There were amateur theatricals, parties, soirées, parties and yet more parties . . . But highest and most costly among the entertainments he shared with his friends was an obsessive interest in, and love of, hunting.

The founder of the South Devon Hunt, George Templer – who

kept his own pack of hounds at Stover – and his friends hunted some three or four days a week in season. Many are the tales that have crept into local folklore. He rode hard and well with no inhibitions. Jumping the tollgates on Shaldon Bridge, keeping his own pack of foxes, dressing a pet monkey in a pink coat and strapping the animal to a horse, to accompany him while hunting – all these colourful titbits of gossip reveal a degree of playfulness in Templer perhaps not entirely conducive to running a successful business, or even maintaining his spending power.

Having to sell both his business and his home to the Duke of Somerset in 1829 must almost have broken George's heart, as the following lines reveal:

'Stover, farewell! Still fancy's hand shall trace
Thy pleasures past in all their former grace;
And I will wear and cherish, though we part,
The dear remembrance ever at my heart.'

But resilience was part of this complex man's character, and after a year spent abroad, he was back in Devon, establishing himself as the chief agent in his old company and building a grand new house at Sandford Orleigh, not far from Stover. Again, things went against him. It was not only his mishandling of business matters that brought the quarries to eventual cessation of work, but contracts were lost. George Templer died after a hunting accident in 1843, to be buried in Teigngrace church, built by his father, James, near the old family home of Stover. Quarrying continued at Haytor into the 1880s, but the granite tramway was no longer used as alternative transport came into being.

Today the quarries behind Haytor, once full of men, noise and primitive machinery, are peaceful, empty places. Nature has softened the clean-cut rock faces and laid green fingers over the littered debris of a forgotten industry. Stone and broken timbers offer habitats for myriad plants and insects. Rainwater has collected in depressions in the ground and in summer jewelled dragonflies dart and hover there.

The whole area of Haytor and its silent quarries has now gained a new importance, even surpassing George Templer's great achievement, for conservation has become the underlying motivation, rather than the exploitation of the rock for commercial gain. Much of the surviving tramway on the open moorland is now scheduled as an Ancient Monument. Every year visitors in their thousands climb the great slopes of the downs – where that noisy celebration once took place – to explore the old quarries and all that they contain.

Because of this ever-growing interest, and to show appreciation of the important historical connection, the Templer Way, a public walk following the path of the old tramway, has been researched and developed.

This eight mile long route starts at Haytor, exploring the quarries, where the remains of the remarkable stone tramway, with its sidings and points, still lie. Then it descends, passing through Yarner Wood, Lowerdown and Bovey Tracey, and going through the grounds of Stover House – these days a country park, the house itself now a school – then continues on to what remains of the canal at Ventiford. The walk follows the river Teign, before reaching its destination, the port of Teignmouth.

In a world of technology that surely he could never have envisaged, it is good to know that the history of the tramway lives on – one man's dream, captured in granite.

Ghosts Galore at Berry Pomeroy Castle

If ever a castle deserved its reputation as being the most haunted in Devon, surely it has to be the ruins at Berry Pomeroy. Over the centuries many generations have lived, loved, perhaps hated, and no doubt sought happiness before dying here. No wonder the ghost stories mount up.

Approached from the village, 3 miles from Totnes, the tree-lined drive of the castle descends in a forebodingly secret fashion until – suddenly – there it is . . . a gaunt, ruined medieval gatehouse with curtain wall and tower which almost, but not quite, hides the view of the handsome Tudor mansion built within its derelict courtyard. Two ruins for the price of one – and ghosts galore. A truly fascinating and spectacular place, whether one believes in ghosts or not.

But Berry has another and less sinister reputation – that of having been the home of just two families throughout its long life. When you consider that the first house was already in existence when the Domesday survey was taken in 1086, the astonishment grows.

Who were those early householders? Henry de la Pomeraye was a Norman, rewarded – as was the custom – with vast gifts of land, after the Conquest. He was given the manor at Berry, and his descendants remained there until the 16th century.

The medieval gatehouse shows signs of added fortification, including gunloops and the provision of a portcullis. These were added in the 14th century, when French raiders menaced Devon's coast. But the house already had its own natural protection – an

unassailable site on a wooded clifftop with a precipitous descent beneath. And it was over this cliff that two Pomeroy brothers, armoured and heavily armed, galloped, charging along the north terrace before leaping their horses over the brink to their deaths, rather than succumb to besieging enemies. This tale has come down over the years, hazy and horrific, perhaps almost unbelievable – but the terrifying drama was actually re-enacted one night not so long ago, when two friends of the author, with ghost-watcher Deryck Seymour, heard the unmistakable sounds of desperate hooves, clanging armour, shouts and threats, before an awful, ensuing silence.

The lifestyle of those early Pomeroys was simple and rough, yet it had a certain primitive charm that contrasts sharply with our own complicated world. Castle walls would have been hung with tapestries and embroideries in the attempt to lessen the chill of damp stone. Herbs and rushes were strewn on pounded earth floors. Animal skins covered beds, and huge fires roared in the hall, where lord and lady sat at their high table, eating vast quantities of home-produced food, while waited on by their servants. But while we might delight in the thought of roasted boar, venision, swan and the occasional peacock for supper, perhaps it is as well not to linger on thoughts of hygiene – or rather the lack of it.

As the years passed, new ideas came into being and comfort in the home increased, as well as better facilities. The great hall was eventually given a ceiling, enabling lord and lady and the family to retreat upstairs, leaving the hoi polloi below. The solar was a dignified, comfortable room, with bedchambers leading out of it. Downstairs, however, the scullions were still less favoured, often sleeping on pallets outside the master's door, or lying with the dogs as close to the ashes of the dying fire as safety allowed.

At some point a terrible hatred and envy grew between two sisters, Margaret and Eleanor Pomeroy, when both fell in love with the same man. Eleanor, the stronger of the two, imprisoned sister Margaret in the dungeon at the base of one of the towers of the medieval dwelling. What happened to her is best left to the imagination, but going down the unevenly-trodden stone circular stair into the place of her incarceration stirs the senses into vivid thoughts of suffering. Slow starvation, continual gloom, and lack of sunlight, engendering possible claustrophobia, added to decreasing hope, must surely have hastened poor Margaret's cruel death.

Today, she is said to haunt the fatal spot, and who can blame her? Revenge is sweet – she is the famous White Lady, who, with streaming hair, has been seen by many visitors, heard by some, and merely sensed by others, in the dungeon. Once she appeared to a terrified investigator after a blinding flash of light. Another visitor just caught a glimpse of her skirt as she climbed the stairs towards the stone door that would never open . . .

The 16th century saw the end of the Pomeroy dynasty at Berry, for they sold their property to the great Seymour family. Now a new age, with exciting Renaissance inspiration, lifted old Berry from its medieval twilight, creating within the castle shell a tall, elegant and beautiful house – a suitable setting for great Sir Edward Seymour.

Sir Edward was the elder brother of Jane Seymour, King Henry's VIII's third wife. The mother of Edward VI, Henry's only son, Jane died soon after the baby's birth. When, aged ten, Edward became King, her brother became the most important man in the realm, Lord Protector and regent of the infant king.

No doubt seeking a new home suitable for his elevated rank, Edward Seymour bought Berry in 1547 and planned an impressive mansion, the most ambitious and fascinating part of which was to be the loggia. The Reverend John Prince, a vicar of the parish, writing in 1701, described this as ' . . . a noble walk . . . arched over with curiously carved freestone, supported on the forepart by several pillars.'

Today we can see a depiction of this handsomely-planned Tudor building, with resplendent state rooms, sweeping staircases, linking passages, and kitchens tucked away at the side, by courtesy of English Heritage. Since 1981 an archaeological team has carried out consolidation work. Much new information has been gathered, resulting in a clear picture of the great mansion as it originally was.

No doubt the Seymours intended to reside in splendour and with far more comfort than their Pomeroy predecessors, but their sojourn was short. Although a man of great ability, the unfortunate Lord Protector was schemed against by powerful enemies, disgraced, finally brought to trial and executed on Tower Hill in 1552. His son, another Edward, succeeded him and work continued on the house, but the Lord Protector's ambitious plans were never brought to fruition. Perhaps lack of funds prevented further building, for much of his estate was confiscated after his trial. The Seymours, however, continued to live in their half-finished mansion until 1690, when the house began the gradual decline into ruination from which it has only recently been saved.

Why did they leave? One possibility is that it must have been highly inconvenient, living in such a dilapidated home, particularly as they had others, dotted all over the country. For whatever reason, they moved to Wiltshire, and so Berry was abandoned.

After that the ruins were frequently robbed of stone by local builders and farmers, and the buildings slowly fell apart. It has been suggested that the house had suffered earlier damage during a Civil War siege, or that lightning struck, even that it was burned down, but the truth remains unknown. One can only conjecture as to what really happened.

In romantic Victorian times the ruins attracted hordes of visitors, and the already rich lode of folklore was added to. Today Berry still sends shivers up the spines of eager ghost-seekers.

Some people have said that the mere atmosphere of the place repels them, even before they reach the ruins. So called 'cold-spots' in the woodland have been reported. There is a panic-stricken feeling of evil. Photographs obstinately refuse to be developed. Visiting dogs are too scared to approach the castle. These are the more general intimations of the local paranormal – specific details are even more interesting.

Chilling faces have been spotted in the upstairs window of St Margaret's Tower, a feeling of panic and torture experienced in the gatehouse dungeon, and dim lights seen traversing the rampart walk topping the medieval curtain wall. The White Lady continues to haunt the tower, but there is also a Blue Lady, whose appearance dates from the end of the 18th century, after unsavoury tales of family incest wove themselves into the existing threads of folklore. She is said to have beckoned from the top of a high, ruined wall; a visitor – a young, impressionable man – climbed up as far as possible, only to fall as the stonework crumbled. He saved himself from death by what seemed a near-miracle. The Blue Lady clearly enjoyed luring men to their deaths.

And the ubiquitous Black Dog also haunts Berry. Seen in so many parts of the county, here it crosses the woodland, menacing all who see it, adding yet another twist of terror to the old tales.

Berry Pomeroy today, newly restored and offering a welcome that visitors will appreciate, is spectacular and fascinating. And even though its sightless eye-sockets of derelict windows and charred stonework ruins of once blazing fireplaces still speak of sinister, spectre-ridden goings on, that is only one side of the coin.

I prefer to think of the ghosts of Berry Pomeroy as a romantic, late Victorian writer did, when he described them as 'Shouts of revelry by night, the baying of hounds eager for the chase, the blare of trumpets assembling hawking parties, the sudden arming of retainers for war or foray, the impatient neighing of bit-champing war horses, and, above all, the merry laughter of the fairest dames and damsels in England . . . '

With all that in mind, I can even imagine Margaret and Eleanor happily living out their remote, intriguing lives, before a certain handsome stranger came, to destroy for ever the innocent dreams they must once have shared.

13

The Undercliff – A Secret Path

On Christmas Eve in 1839, the cliffs between Axmouth and Lyme Regis collapsed. At that time, despite hazy historical memories of previous cliff-falls, there were two small cottages established in the undercliff below Dowlands Farm. That night their inhabitants awoke at midnight to hear terrifying noises. Was it an earthquake?

Rocks, grinding as they fell against each other in the process of finding a firm base. The noise was likened to sheets tearing . . . in the blackness of a winter night it was a truly horrifying sound. Inside, the cottage floors flew up towards falling ceilings. One cottage was entirely demolished, but somehow the inhabitants escaped.

Further along the cliffs, coastguards' lanterns highlighted rocks rising out of the churning sea, close to shore. This newly-created reef extended nearly half a mile in length. It continued to rise and the men fled, only to discover that the fields bordering the clifftops were breaking into great gulleys and ravines, across which they had to leap as they ran to safety.

By next day over 20 acres of land had parted company with the mainland, some of it coming to rest halfway down the cliff. The remainder of the fall sank into a huge chasm nearly three-quarters of a mile long. Gradually the truth hit the villagers – no earthquake, but an almighty landslip.

The disaster was eventually explained as being due to the geology of the area. The chalky top layers of the cliff along that stretch of East Devon coast become water-logged as they absorb spring water and seasonal rain. Lower down the strata of clay is not absorbent and so the wet masses slide about, failing to find a safer foundation upon which to come to rest. Smaller landslips had been taking place here for nearly 200 years; this one, in 1839, was memorable, turning the landscape into the one we see today.

As spring came that year, so nature began to spread itself over the bare rocks, boulders, cliff-faces and ravines. And it became obvious to the men who explored and used the region – men from the clifftop estates of Rousdon House and Bindon Manor, woodmen, smugglers, coastguards, farmers seeking new uses for the land they had so disastrously lost – that this was a place where everything grew . . . and grew. Sheltered from the cold winds, facing south, and with the slant of the displaced land uptilted towards the sun, the Undercliff soon grew lush and abundant, as if offering some compensation for all the trouble it had caused.

In the Philpot Museum in Lyme Regis, there is an engraving, *View of the Great Chasm of the Axmouth Landslip* by William Dawson, which shows the state of the Undercliff the year following the landslip. It also commemorates an amazing occasion – the reaping of a field of wheat which had fallen from farmland above, landed in one workable piece and continued to grow and ripen.

In this evocative little picture you can see visitors wandering – at great risk, one would imagine – around the moon-like, bare and dangerous landscape. In the field a reaping party is at work, and from old records we are told that the locals made this an occasion to remember – the 25th August 1840. Local dignitaries and bands of musicians made their way over the fallen rocks to the field, and there twelve especially selected young people – six of each sex – dressed in blue and white, with sickles decorated with flowers and ribbons, commenced the harvest.

Alas, they were only enthusiastic amateurs; after one young maid cut her hand, the professionals took over, while a crowd of 6,000 onlookers watched and applauded. Tokens of the occasion were given out in the form of silver sickles, for it was definitely a day to remember, and to celebrate man's superiority over nature.

But this superiority was not to last long. Once nature got into her seasonal stride, profligate growth proved more than man could cope with, stubborn as he was. Sheep were brought down to graze the rich grass and pigs rooted in the fast-growing woodland – but only temporarily. Smugglers, though, continued their long tradition of carrying booty secretly through the winding, dangerous paths, followed by Preventive Officers. And eventually visitors came – Alfred, Lord Tennyson, was one. In his wake tourism developed, one astute local lady eagerly offering cream teas to the weary wanderers . . .

Nature slowly, but surely, won the uneven fight, banishing all save experts and committed walkers. For today the Undercliff has become a National Nature Reserve, and its 6-mile walk, from the Axe Estuary to Lyme Regis, is part of the South West Coast Path. The track must be strictly adhered to, and written permission is needed for experts studying geology, wild life and so on, to explore any distance away from it. The Undercliff is uneven, dangerous ground, full of overgrown crevices, ledges and invisible ravines. There are boggy areas and freshwater pools, rocky scrub and bare cliff-faces that threaten further falls.

Walking the winding, up-and-down path can be safe enough, however, although not entirely without hazard. Accidents may all too easily occur. There are enough fresh falls of cream-coloured rocks and scree to remind one of past history. But, having given due warning of the possible dangers, it must be said that to walk in the Undercliff is to make, without doubt, a magic journey that will remain in the mind for a long time.

It is a land of sea mist and drifting cloud, of filtered sunlight in summertime, of peephole views showing glimpses of glittering, rocking sea far below, and awe-inspiring towers of dull grey cliff above. Through the immense ash trees, vigorous climbing plants thrust their light-seeking ropes and trails ever heavenward. Here wild flowers grown finer and earlier than elsewhere. Foxes, badgers, and roedeer live secretly within the undergrowth that masks myriad tiny trackways. To reptiles, mammals and insects this is a haven where they may live, safe from man's depredations. Fossils of great beauty and antiquity abound, concealed from all but the expert's eye. And here and there a homely apple tree or a clump of herbs reminds one of the people who once had their cottage homes in this strange, dangerous, yet beautiful place.

A primeval silence reigns, of which the music of songbirds and the insistent soughing of sea winds seem an integral part. The Undercliff is a many-faceted whole and one is constantly aware that nature has spread her equilibrium all around. Seeding, growth, ripeness and decay have their little moments, and then give way to a fresh cycle of life. All is in balance, undeterred by man.

John Fowles, the renowned novelist, lives locally. He has celebrated the Undercliff in his book, *The French Lieutenant's Woman*, and also written a foreword to Elaine Frank's magnificent *Sketchbook*, which so beautifully illustrates the area.

Many visitors have already walked this small part of the South West Coast Path and many more will do so. But, whereas in most old tales it is the people of a region who create interest, here in the Axmouth Undercliff it is the land itself, powerful and memorable, that fills the mind of the walker turning down from the field footpath into the first slope of woodland.

Cruel cliffs stare down. Below, the sea ripples. Birds call, and one dives into a green wonderland. Truly, a magical experience, never to be forgotten.

NOTE: Would-be walkers are advised to obtain – from a local information centre – the Countryside Commission leaflet, East Devon Guide 5, *The Axe Estuary to Lyme Regis*, before undertaking the walk. It is vital to understand that there are no paths leading either seawards or to the clifftop along the way. Once you start you must either return the same way or continue. Written permission must be sought before any exploration of the land away from the Coast Path may be undertaken.

14

A Sweet Singer of Songs

'**O** Romeo, Romeo! wherefore art thou Romeo?' 'Look 'roun' the corner and ee'll see un, maid!'

Such catcalls and even bawdier comments held no terror for twelve year old Maria Foote, making her début as Juliet in her father's theatre in the dock area of Plymouth in the early years of the 19th century.

A natural performer, she was an attractive child and knew her own worth, even at that age. And the shrieks and laughter of the smelly, smoky crowds filling the theatre merely acted as a spur to her ambition. One day she would go to London and become famous . . .

The rough, shabbily-dressed audience had elbowed and pushed its way into the theatre with noisy abandon earlier that evening. A smell of greasepaint and stale air had greeted them, but they were a raffish lot, mostly labourers from the dockyard, some artisans, and a few sailors ashore, enjoying the company of the local girls.

Somehow they had found the entrance fee. But whether earned, borrowed or stolen, the idea of affording two shillings and sixpence for a seat in a box was too ludicrous for any of them to entertain. The hands that had delved into threadbare pockets came out with only the sixpence, providing standing room in the gods. This was no disappointment, for from that vantage point, high at the back of the auditorium, they could actively, and often physically, participate in the actual performance. Insults, bottles, oranges, and other missiles were thrown onto the stage, often hitting the actors, which, of course, was the intent. For these wild audiences looked forward to an evening of riotous, energetic noise and horseplay, and made sure they got it.

'This house,' commented a theatrical critic at the end of the previous century, 'is a nightly scene of riot and debauchery.' And even by the time Georgian days had ended, and the young Victoria was on her throne, the Dock Theatre in Plymouth was still persisting in its shocking ways.

But on stage Juliet continued to woo her Romeo, both players raising their voices and dodging the oranges when necessary. Nothing mattered but the play. Maria Foote had been born into the theatre, the daughter of Samuel Freeman, an ex-army officer who changed names with his switch of profession, when he took on the Dock's management. Later, he renamed it the Theatre Royal, hoping, no doubt, to remove its unsavoury reputation.

With such hard-earned experience of local repertory behind her, Maria did, indeed, get to London by the time she was 17, her first part setting her on the stage of the Covent Garden Theatre. By that time she had blossomed into a beautiful woman. Good parts came her way, and she was kept busy, both as actress and singer, though there seems to have been a little doubt as to her true worth. She has been wryly described as 'a successful singer – or at least she sang songs sweetly, if not very well.'

But without doubt, her greatest performance was as the plaintiff in a notorious breach of promise case in 1824, when her love affairs were revealed in full detail to a scandalised, but delighted, countrywide audience.

Maria had formed a liasion with Colonel Berkely, eldest son of the Earl of Berkely, and was said to be living under his protection during their long engagement, for marriage was decreed not to take place until he succeeded to the title. During those years of waiting, Maria produced two children by the Colonel, and perhaps would have discreetly maintained their relationship, had she not been introduced, through her lover, to the circle of dandified young beaux lording it in London society. Here she met a certain Joseph Hayne – nicknamed Pea Green because of the colour of his flamboyant suits – and completely captivated the young man. The attraction was mutual, but despite his passion, not to mention his extreme wealth, their affair was brought to a quick end when the enamoured Pea Green proposed marriage,

only to be sharply acquainted by the irate Colonel Berkely of the true state of things.

Perhaps at this point one might sympathise with poor Maria. It could not have been easy, waiting for ever for her aristocratic Colonel to keep his promise. Would his Papa never die? And here was Pea Green, with his fortune and his youth – three years her junior and seemingly without a care in the world – not to mention his status in uppercrust London society, which she had been denied as the Colonel's secret mistress. What a temptation to an emotional, ambitious and beautiful woman . . .

The Colonel, perhaps with a mind to ridding himself of an unfaithful alliance, then suggested taking custody of his children, and so Pea Green, smitten all over again, made a second offer of marriage, which was eagerly accepted. In fact, he continued to make these proposals, and then withdrew them, as he and Maria went from one broken engagement to the next. After his last change of heart, and no doubt feeling very bitter about the loss of his agreed offer to settle £40,000 upon her and any children of the forthcoming marriage, Maria took him to court for breach of promise, demanding damages of £10,000.

After a much publicised case in which both her disastrous relationships were revealed to the public, she won the day. Did she bring her skills into court, acting out the abandoned, pathetic woman? Most likely, for the Attorney-General said, at the end of the case, that he could not trust himself to use the language he thought sufficient to express his detestation of the Colonel's behaviour.

He also said that Joseph Hayne appeared to be a public fop, not knowing his own mind from one day to the next. In fact, Maria Foote emerged from court as a sadly wronged, but righteous woman, and was awarded damages of £3,000.

Although the amount was smaller than she had hoped for, Maria must have realised the far greater worth of the public sympathy that she had won. She returned to the stage, only leaving it in 1832 when she married the eccentric 4th Earl of Harrington, from then on successfully playing the part of his Countess for the remainder of her days.

But before that aristocratic marriage took place, Maria's acting career prospered, and at one of her many appearances in Exeter – in 1824, the year of her court case – a bill declared that:

'The Public are respectfully informed that MISS FOOTE
will perform in Exeter one night, on her way through
from Plymouth.'

No doubt Maria gave the performance of her life that evening, having already experienced to the full the title of the play, which was *Lover's Vows*.

15

To Right a Wrong

Extraordinary rumours had been flying around the South
Hams for weeks. On a cold, wet November morning in 1943
the truth was revealed.

In East Allington church the Lord Lieutenant of Devon
explained to the villagers, who had been called to the meeting,
that the three mile long Slapton Sands, together with its surrounding farmlands and villages, was to be evacuated. The
similarity between the coastline of the area and the Normandy
coast, soon to be the target of assault by Allied troops, prompted
the use of Slapton and its environs for rehearsals of fullscale battle
exercises. Now American troops were to occupy the evacuated
villages. And that wasn't all . . .

'You have six weeks in which to move out,' said Lord Fortescue,
his words falling into an unbelieving silence.

Later that day he gave the same message to an equally stunned
audience in Stokenham church. And on Monday similar meetings
were held at Blackawton and Slapton.

Reactions were hostile. Leave our homes? Our farms – the best
lands in Devon? Madness! Can't be done! But once initial shock
wore off, patriotism overcame any lingering outrage. If giving up
the land to the Yanks would bring the war to a quicker end, then it
would be worth all the pain, muddle and anxiety that such a move
must entail.

Many of the elderly villagers had never been out of the South
Hams. They were shocked and bewildered at the mere thought of
having to leave. Where would they go? What would happen to the
farmland, the houses, their livestock – their pets? Who would pay
for the upheaval? Would anyone help with all the consequent

problems? And how could they possibly manage to find new homes and move all their belongings in just six short weeks?

The South Hams is a region of small hamlets and farms. Its gentle hills are appealingly beautiful, and it is a land of rich, fertile pastures, for centuries a heartland of Devon, famed for its herds of Ruby Reds and South Devon cattle. But in 1943 the land, which had been worked for so many generations, was willingly handed over to an Allied mechanised army, intent on preparing for the final, deadly attack on the enemy in Europe. Live ammunition, heavy transport and constant exercises were bound to inflict terrible damage – no wonder the 3,000 inhabitants of those beloved pastures, stone farmhouses and cob cottages shed tears at the thought of leaving.

The Government undertook to pay expenses, rents, and to give free storage of possessions. Relevant ministries and civil organisations were put at the disposal of the villagers. But, without doubt, the ordinary business of moving house and dealing with the magnitude of personal problems lay in the capable hands of the Women's Voluntary Service, who listened to fears and anger, advised about worries, large and small, and sympathetically persuaded stubborn old people to change their minds about refusing to leave their homes. The ladies of the WVS are justly remembered with respect and gratitude for the part they played in the South Hams evacuation.

Those of the evacuated villagers still alive will never forget how they moved, that December. Livestock was either sold or taken to a friendly farmer out of the assault area, to be looked after and pastured for the period of evacuation – hopefully put at nine months. Small cottage bedrooms were willingly cleared in villages bordering the area to make space for another family moving in. Some people left the South Hams never to return. But most of the 3,000 were somehow absorbed in and around the neighbouring villages, just beyond the limits of the evacuation area.

Heartache and distress were the order of the day, with old pets being put down, tame hens chased, caught, and put in boxes to be taken to the new home, sacks of the last lumps of coal heaved onto boys' shoulders, and everybody packing their valuables into

boxes, bags, buckets and brown paper parcels. Prams, wheel-barrows, birdcages – they all had to go.

One old villager had a heart attack as she left her cottage, and many more suffered in other ways, for not everyone had the strength, either of body or spirit, to start a new life, or even to plan a return; for who knew how long the war could go on?

Not only were private homes being packed up, but the village churches were also denuded of their treasures. Priceless 15th-century carved wooden screens were taken down, dismantled and packed away with ancient silver plate and other valuables. Farm machinery rumbled away down the lanes to safety, countless chimney fires were let out for the last time, and homes were finally emptied of both belongings and owners. And while all this was happening, the six weeks flew past increasingly quickly.

It was a time of lamenting exodus, followed at once by a noisy, vigorous and optimistic arrival.

American troops were stationed all over Devon, and now the emptied villages were filled with friendly, extrovert, gum-chewing GIs, eager to get on with the job. They drove their jeeps and heavy transport around the area, constantly losing themselves among the narrow, twisting lanes, from which all signposts had long since vanished. Hedges were removed when they got in the way, bends in roads straightened out. Those evacuated villagers who watched the goings-on from peep-holes in the barbed wire fence could hardly credit what was happening to their homeland. But the Yanks understood how their evicted hosts must feel. Many were the kindly unofficial handouts, the bars of candy, the baskets of fruit, which the war-torn English had not seen for the last four years.

Slowly, tales of live ammunition wrecking their houses and farms seeped through the barrier of 'Careless Talk Costs Lives', but the villagers could do nothing. And when rumours of 'accidents' were also relayed through the grapevine of local gossip, they simply shook their heads and got on with the day's living. It was wartime and anything could happen.

That certain accidents had indeed occurred was a fact. But the truth of the final and most terrible accident was not to be revealed until many years after the end of the war – in fact, long after the evacuated area had been rehabilitated and returned to the villagers.

The war had been won, and life continued, picking up old threads and creating difficult new ones; in 1954 the American government had put up a monument to thank residents for evacuating their villages during the D-day rehearsals. Then a local guest-house owner, Ken Small, began beachcombing along the great curve of Slapton Sands, and found not only 3d bits, old half-crowns and jewellery, but disturbing pieces of militaria. Live and spent bullets appeared, cap badges, buttons, shrapnel, shellcases and mines. Even pieces of military vehicles. He sensed something very wrong. Everyone knew now that lives had been lost here during the assault exercises, but not how many. Local tales were of little help, though there were vague rumours of bodies being buried under cover of darkness and kept secret.

Ken Small was filled with a resolution to find out the truth of these tales. And then a fisherman friend told him of 'something' lying on the sea bed, three-quarters of a mile off shore.

Divers inspecting the 'something' reported that it was an American Sherman tank, intact and fitted with equipment that plainly adapted it for use at sea. Now local memories were exercised, and began to dig a little deeper. Yes, the bay had been subjected to heavy shelling and bombing. And there had been a half-believed secret, all but forgotten now, in the excitement of returning home and working the cherished land back to its previous fertility. That secret – something about Exercise Tiger. . .

Ken Small then embarked on what was to become the obsession of his life. His first object was to lift the tank from the sea bed and install it somewhere nearby, where it would be a memorial to lost American troops, for by now he was convinced that the numbers of lives lost had been hushed-up by the authorities.

It was a business fraught with denials, ignored letters and telephone calls, much procrastination and everlasting delay. But, eventually, as a result of persistent and dedicated enquiries, both in England and America, he learned the truth about Exercise Tiger. It took him another ten years to reveal the whole story.

'On the night of 28th April, 1944, patrolling German gunboats surprised a landing exercise at sea. The engagement was brief, but 749 U.S. soldiers and sailors were killed.'

These shocking facts, simply recorded for a recent service of commemoration, cannot possibly register the suffering that they engendered. Only as Ken Small managed to contact surviors of the disaster, and families of those who lost their lives, and to persuade the authorities to reveal the truth, were the personal experiences of agony and bitterness made public. Even the undeniable fact that the practices under fire in the evacuated area had played a large part in the success of the D-day landings, can never wholly erase the tragedy of all those lives being sacrificed.

It is entirely due to Ken Small's relentless pursuit of his obsession to discover the truth, that today Exercise Tiger has been made public knowledge, and its victims given the memorial that is their due.

On Thursday, 28th April 1994, a memorial service was held on Slapton Sands in honour of the men who died in Exercise Tiger. Officials from British and American embassies and militia joined with former servicemen, relatives and friends of the dead and local people who remembered the dark days of war, 50 years before. Within sight of the spot where so many young men died, the last post was sounded, followed by *The Stars and Stripes*, and then the standard of the Normandy veterans was lowered in respect. A moving, simple ceremony, heralding other events which took place throughout the following few weeks, to mark the 50th anniversary of D-Day – 6th June 1944.

Now the evacuation of the eight villages around the Slapton area has filtered away into past memory, to be recalled only infrequently. Once again the rich farmlands are producing fruitful harvests. Beauty has returned, and with it a sense of well-being. The curving, glittering shingle of Slapton Sands is edged with wild flowers, and on its landward side freshwater Slapton Ley hosts myriad forms of flora and fauna. This beautiful view, in summer full of happy visitors and sunlight, gives no indication of its dark and turbulent past.

But at the Torcross end, a man passes his time beside the Sherman tank memorial. Dressed in his customary black, Ken Small sells copies of his book. *The Forgotten Dead*, from his parked car. Mild-mannered and friendly, it's difficult to realise he is an historical figure, the resolute man whose persistence eventually raised the Sherman tank from the seabed, to create a memorial to the American dead. A man who tried to put right a great wrong, and succeeded.

Ask him about Exercise Tiger, and you will see the entrancing, sea-lapped beach from an entirely new viewpoint.

16

Men from the Hills

L iving among remote and wild parts of Devon in the past were various small communities of savage and lawless men. They were horse thieves, footpads, criminals, deserters from ill-founded causes and desperadoes of all sorts who, with their women and children, were on the run from authority.

Many were cattle rustlers, stealing their neighbours' stock in order to survive in places where the landscape was inhospitable and the moorland incapable of growing crops. No neighbouring farmer, if he valued his life and property, would betray their whereabouts. Indeed, no one would even dare complain when precious stock disappeared into the fastness of concealing valleys behind the distant hills. In those days the law had no long arm to reach so far.

In the 17th and 18th centuries, and even in more recent times, a reverberation of fear clung to certain names when they were spoken. The hell-raising Doones of Exmoor and the red-haired Gubbins clan of Lydford will be long remembered. And the scythestone men of the Blackdown Hills, who were also wild but redeemed themselves by working honestly for their living, hold a place in Devon's history, too, for each small group has a tale worth the telling.

* * *

'The Doones are coming . . . !'

That cry, among the coombes and scattered farms of northern Exmoor during the early 17th century, was enough to make mothers snatch their children indoors and men to reach for their guns.

If the little posse of horsemen, in their rough animal-skin coats, galloped past, all would be well – until the next raid, when sheep, cattle, even women, might be taken back to the ruined medieval settlement at Badgery which the outlaws had made their home. Such raids were frequent and, together with highway robbery, were the means by which the Doones survived the harsh life of the remote moorland.

Although their historical origin is in some doubt, with various suggestions that they were exiles from Scotland, or in later years survivors of the Monmouth rebellion of 1685, one authority believes them to have been merely a gang of desperate men fleeing from the law, who settled on Exmoor in the early 1600s. Several savage murders were committed down the years, as well as the everyday occurrence of stealing stock, and although at first the lack of communication of the period ensured their survival, eventually their terrible deeds forced the men of Exmoor to ride against them. The settlement at Badgery was overcome, and the Doones fled.

Their callous exploits might well have slowly been forgotten had not the author R.D. Blackmore published, in 1869, his novel, *Lorna Doone*. He openly stated that he was basing his story on the handed-down folktales of the Doones, and that fact, together with his recognisable descriptions of local scenery, soon established both his heroine, Lorna, and the home of her wicked abductors in Doone Valley, in the world's mind.

Today, visitors in their thousands walk the moorland path to Badgery Water, looking for the famous landmarks of Blackmore's tale – the water slide where handsome Jan Ridd first found the kidnapped girl, the precipitous Doone-gate through which Carver Doone and his savage men rode out to terrorise the countryside, and the humps and bumps of overgrown masonry that are all that remains of the ancient settlement. Plovers Farm and Oare Church, where Lorna was shot on her wedding day, are other points of interest on the pilgrimage, which happily ends with a splendid Devon cream tea in the pretty Lorna Doone village of Malmsmead.

Among all this gentle nostalgia perhaps it is a little unkind, but necessary, to remember the true nature of the Doones. Many terrible tales have been handed down over the intervening centuries, but their final claim to notoriety, and the one which ended their reign of terror, was the murder of a child, whose mother they were carrying off.

Laughing as they rode away, they shouted back a rhyme which has passed into folklore:

'Child, if they ask who killed thee –
Say it was the Doones of Badgery.'

* * *

Said by folklore to have been red-haired, naked and savage, the Gubbins tribe established their lawless stronghold in the gorge of the river Lyd, in the village of Lydford on the northern fringe of Dartmoor, some unspecified time in the distant past.

In 1650, Thomas Fuller wrote about them with great distaste. 'Some 200 years since, two strumpets being with child, fled thither to hide themselves, to whom certain lewd fellows resorted, and this was their first original.' He described their name as inferring shame and disgrace, originating in the useless shavings of fish, called gubbings.

Fuller went on to detail the Gubbinses' lifestyle, which he said was similar to that of swine. They lived in hovels and caves, he said, breeding amongst themselves until their numbers reached many hundreds. Their language was 'the dross of the vulgar Devonian', which no one else understood. They lived on sheep stolen from the moor, robbed travellers, and were beyond the powers of the law, being able to run faster than many horses. When threatened, they banded fiercely together. 'Offend one,' Fuller declared, 'and all will revenge his quarrel.'

Lydford Gorge must have retained echoes of such depravity long after their eventual disappearance, and the name of their leader, Roger Rowle, lives on, commemorated in Rowles Pool. This lies just beyond the pothole called the Devil's Cauldron at the head of the gorge, where the river Lyd rising some three miles north-east, comes swirling into the precipitous ravine, which was originally gouged out of the rock 450,000 years ago.

This spectacular gorge is now in the safe, caring hands of the National Trust, and visitors can walk the mile and a half long river path from one end of the valley to the other. After rain the rocky tracks can be slippery, but handrails are provided, and the experience of descending into the tree-lined depths is worth a little effort. The canopies of branches hang overhead, and within the green gloom, highlighted in summer with dappled sunlight, all sorts of delights await the observant visitor. Flora and fauna are rich and varied, and at the far end of the gorge the magnificent backdrop of the famous White Lady waterfall thunders down, in a mist-ridden 100 ft drop.

The Gubbins clan, we are told, was eventually wiped out by inbreeding and its depraved way of life, and yet. . . Glance back before leaving this atmospheric spot, and allow your imagination to run loose for a few enchanted moments.

The resident ghost of the White Lady hovers among the misty gown of her falling water, shadows drift imperceptibly as the dimpsey comes down, green foliage stirs and thickens. On the towering rockfaces above, black caves still darken the stone, and time slides away, for at such moments the Gubbinses undoubtedly live on – if only in memory.

* * *

''Tis all over in ten minutes, like the scythestone fair. . .'

So said the Exeter townsfolk some 200 years ago, having watched the small straggle of people, leading their train of ponies and asses, laden panniers sweeping the sides of the narrow lanes, going home to the distant Blackdown Hills.

The scythestone men, as they were called, mined whetstones from the hillside and brought their wares to the annual fair in Exeter's old Waterbeer Street bright and early every May Day. They were there as dawn broke and left before most people had finished their breakfasts. Once the stones were sold there was money for vital groceries and then the little group, which included women and children, roughly dressed in clothes made from animal skins, with thick boots, scuffed and worn, hair long and wild to match the men's beards, travelled the ten miles back to their camp, high up among steep escarpments and plunging valleys of the Blackdown Hills. Reaching the foothills of the ascending slopes, the groceries in the panniers had to be pushed deeper, for here, on the fringe of the rich, red-hearted farmlands, the scythestone men collected as much good earth as they could carry to help fertilise the thin soil of their hillside gardens.

Hard-working and as self-sufficient as was possible, surely the scythestone men did not deserve the reputation they earned among their neighbours in the remote, barely inhabited hills – but they were Celts, coming from either Wales or Cornwall and speaking a language no one could understand. Foreigners, the parochial Devonians called them, and so beyond the pale. They were a tough, unfriendly community. A nosy stranger might well be pushed down a handy mineshaft, or into a brekle, as the waste tips were called. Their visits to the local Ponchydown Inn were fraught with hostility and aggression.

The work of whetstone mining was hard, with boys, men, and women as well, digging out level galleries into the hillface, to the length of 300 yards. Cross-galleries, timbered and lit with candles, were added. At one time 24 pits were worked, with 70 people employed and living on rough campsites, on the surrounding hillside. The precious whetstone was taken from the loose topsoil and then roughly dressed with basing hammers at the pit mouth. Dressing the stone raised dust which caused pulmonary illness, and few of the men lived longer than a mere 40 years.

The scythestone men's workings came to an end with the arrival of competition from foreign imports and, later, the invention of carborundum. What happened to the little community is not known for certain, but one theory is that it fell into a nomadic way of life, wandering the Blackdowns and surviving as best it could.

Two gypsy families, the Manleys and the Mullhollands are known to have made the hills their homes in late Victorian times, the men dealing in horses and their women and children making and selling clothes-pegs. The gypsies, claiming Cornish descent, were famous for their rivalry, and when both families were known to be heading for the same village, local police stood firm.

Today, nature has grown over the waste tips and subsiding galleries and the Ponchydown pub has become respectable. But stories of the fierce scythestone men still, occasionally, are given an airing, adding a vivid thread to Devon's rich tapestry of folklore.

17

Travellers along the Way

Like a green tunnel, the narrow lane opens up ahead of the car, high-hedged and mysteriously winding. There is a sense of adventure in driving slowly around the unpredictable twists and corners. In high summer bleached grasses lean out, scattering seeds onto the dusty tarmac below. Tall hedgerow saplings of oak and ash, holly and hazel, let dappled sunlight filter through their shady green canopies, falling like a blessing on the travellers who chance that way. Wild flowers star the overgrown banks.

Some drivers, more used to urban speed, curse at the enforced slowness. Many reverse reluctantly when another car comes around an unexpected corner. But the enlightened few obligingly change gear and creep along, treating the lane with respect, and enjoying the sense of being back in the past. For they are driving down an ancient Devon lane, and history is all about them.

The first roads of Devon were rough animal tracks following the contours of the land. Then came small, dark, quick-eyed Bronze Age men, treading hard the faint paths along the ridges of the high hills, felling trees and moving boulders to make the trackways clearer. These settlers from the Mediterranean came to Britain nearly 4,000 years ago and farmed the uplands of Devon. In the 3rd century BC they were followed by another wave of immigrants from Brittany. These were the Celts, who had more sophisticated iron weapons and tools, and who enlarged the roads already in existence.

Thus began the local Devon traffic. Cattle moving from pasture to pasture, blacksmiths travelling to the next settlement, traders hawking their wares, and warriors on tribal forays marching on their enemies.

When the Romans arrived, they built their straight military roads by utilising whatever tracks they found and filling in the necessary gaps as they went. The road from Exeter to Torquay, the A38, which becomes the A380 after Telegraph Hill, is a fine example of a prehistoric route developed over the centuries and still in use today. The A380 deviates from the old road just before reaching Kingsteignton, but the remnant of Roman road, now a narrow, tree-lined lane, runs down into the hamlet of Sandygate. There it crosses the Colleybrook by a bridge, originally a ford. On the other side is the Sandygate Inn, once called Tom the Piper. Not only traders and drovers, but soldiers, too, came this way nearly 2,000 years ago.

By the 7th century AD, the colonising, fair-haired, farming Anglo-Saxons were busy enlarging the small network of tracks already in existence in Devon, as they cleared huge areas of forest, drained swamps, and moved all possible barriers in order to build new homesteads and villages. Ditches were dug and banks raised to make new boundaries, and between these fertile banks, planted with 'quicksett' – young hawthorn split down the middle and laid horizontally – ran many of the Devon lanes that still entrance – or infuriate – today's visitors.

The Middle Ages, too, made use of prehistoric tracks. Near where the Bronze Age men lived on Dartmoor's unfriendly waste, in their circular, stoned settlements, an ancient path was formed which the monks used, as they travelled from Buckfast Abbey, on the south side of the moor, to Buckland Abbey on the western side. Like the Romans before them, they created this Abbots' Way from established ancient tracks, filling in the gaps as they journeyed. The Abbots' Way has remained a famous trackway across Dartmoor, and is today popular with walkers.

The Way – clearly marked on the OS map of Dartmoor – passes through lanes, green roads, occasional stands of woodland, over stone clapper bridges and across peaty streams and rivers. Relics of past medieval tin mining industrial sites, and earlier Bronze Age homesteads, lie close to it, and there are occasional rough-carved, weathered granite crosses erected by the travelling monks, yesterday's signposts. It is wild, sometimes rocky, always demand-

ing, but beautiful, with only buzzards, a pair of ravens, and perhaps a greeting from a passing rambler, to break the solitude. The monks walked the Way throughout the year, through mist, rain, snow and summer's shimmering heat; a tribute to their stamina and persistence.

In the more populated lowlands of Devon, travel was easier, for the Middle Ages were a time of great colonisation, with new roads joining the ever-growing settlements. Soon main roads were established, linking market towns, and enabling merchandise to travel by trains of pack ponies.

Celia Fiennes, an intrepid 17th-century traveller who rode through Britain, made fascinating comments on all she encountered. She described the transport system of the day, 'All their carriages are here on the backs of horses with sort of hookes like yoakes stand up on each side of a good height, which are the receptacles of their goods, either wood, furze, or lime, or coal or corn, or hay or straw, or what else they convey from place to place. . .'

In Devon these strong pack ponies were bred to a height of 15 hands and trained to carry up to 400 lb loads. They were encouraged to take long strides, but confusion arose whenever two trains met in a narrow lane. And reversing a train of rolling-eyed ponies, loaded to the hilt on both sides, must have been far more traumatic than reversing one's car today.

Other travellers along the way were the drovers, taking their cattle to market with only a dog for company, and gladly stopping at every small hedgerow alehouse that lay beside the rough road. There are still some of the old drove roads to be found, recognisable by the wide grass verges bordering them in places, where the cattle grazed and where the drovers, all other shelter failing, curled up in a blanket under the hedge beside the dog when night fell. It is a fascinating exercise to search for clues which indicate the presence of these old routes, often now incorporated into minor county roads. Sometimes the sight of a stand of dilapidated Scots pine trees bordering the verge beside a remote farm is a guide; these were probably planted as a sign of possible accommodation for both drover and his stock for the night.

Owing to the mixture of rain, flood, mud, dust and flint which made roads nearly impassable, all travel must have been a nightmare in past centuries. Again, Celia Fiennes painted a realistic picture. When she rode from Chudleigh to Plymouth, via Ashburton, she commented later, 'The wayes now become so difficult that one could scarcely pass by each other, even the single horses. And so dirty in many places, and just a track for one horse's feete and the bank on either side so near.'

The repair of these disastrous roads was a parish responsibility, seldom carried out. In the 18th century turnpike trusts were set up to improve matters, whereby the paying of tolls on passing traffic would finance the vital repairs. A general Turnpike Act was enacted in 1773, to speed up the long-drawn-out Parliamentary process needed to pass the many separate acts required to create turnpike trusts for individual roads all over the country.

Under these trusts, small tollhouses were built, usually at crossroads and corners, often projecting out into the road, with semi-octagonal fronts. Beside the house a gate and tollbar remained closed until the necessary charge was collected by the pike-man who lived in the house. Charges ranged from a farthing per head of cattle to sixpence for a carriage horse. Church and funeral traffic was exempt, as were local farm carts and the Royal Mail. In the first years of tollhouses being built, riots occurred, as might well be expected. The idea of having to pay for using a road was not popular.

Many of these attractive old houses can be found today, some restored almost out of recognition, but most still have the projecting front, which is easily spotted. They are sited on the outskirts of villages and towns, and some owners are proud enough of their history to display a board painted with the list of charges.

Following the subsequent improvement of main road conditions in the country due to the turnpike trusts, the early 19th century heralded the era of coach traffic. Now the countryside really began to move.

Along the newly repaired main roads, and also the green lanes, bridleways, and flinty, dusty tracks that remained in their rough states, rumbled the carriages of local dignitaries. Private roads on estates resounded with galloping horses, and in the bigger market towns coaching business became all-important, with the clarion call of the Royal Mail horns now heard throughout the land. Decorated with the royal coat of arms on door panels, these spanking new coaches weighed about a ton. They carried four passengers inside and another four outside with their luggage. At the back sat the guard, the key to the mailbox beneath his boot, and a blunderbuss at the ready.

Coaching days were exciting and dangerous, for these vehicles frequently broke their axles, got stuck in the mud, lamed their horses and even threw occupants into the ditch as they rounded corners too fast. Nothing would stop them, though, for the mail had to get through . . .

Accidents were not the only hazards. It was generally, if

reluctantly, accepted by the travelling public that one's journey might well be interrupted by the thundering of overtaking hooves, and a loud voice demanding 'Your money or your life!' But even when staring down the muzzle of a highwayman's pistol, travellers usually merely sighed as they handed over their valuables. For highwaymen – or 'Knights of the Road', even 'Gentlemen of the High Toby', as newspapers of the time thrillingly described them – were known to be (usually) quite polite. They assured their victims they were driven into this shameful way of life by dire poverty and were known to be most unlikely to use the pistols they brandished with such formidable eloquence.

There had, of course, always been a darker side. . . Not far from Chudleigh, on the Exeter to Plymouth road, a highwayman called Jack Withrington practised his trade. Pursued one day, he hid, unsuccessfully, in the chimney breast of his cottage home. Jack died for his wicked deeds, hanged at Tyburn in 1691; how surprised he would have been to know that his home is now called 'The Highwayman's Haunt'.

The coaching business developed rapidly, and Exeter became the centre of a huge network of coaches travelling up and down the country, with 70 leaving every day, by the 1830s. The famous 'Telegraph' coach left the New London Inn at 5 am and reached London in 17 hours. It was said to be a 'very superior and well-conducted fast coach', enabling its occupants – mostly male – to pass the the time playing whist.

By the late 1800s tourism had come to Devon, and so road transport was all-important, with coach trips in popular demand. The Dolphin Inn, in Bovey Tracey (already publicised as 'The Gateway to Dartmoor') featured in many a photograph of the times, with a large horse-drawn vehicle parked outside its entrance. Expectant passengers, in heavy Victorian clothing, sat inside, and on top of, the coach. The route was nearly always up the newly-cut county road, passing spectacular Becky Falls and then making for the twin peaks of Hay Tor, the most popular venue on the eastern side of Dartmoor. Owing to the steepness of these moorland hills, gentlemen passengers were asked to leave their seats and walk, to assist the horses.

Macadamisation was a godsend to the transport business, and travel in general. Named after the Scots engineer John Loudon McAdam, this process involved tar being used to bind small stones into an even and durable surface, and so by the start of the 20th century roads were ready for the astounding explosion of vehicles released by the creation of the internal combustion engine. Along these new, smooth and enticing routes came an ever-increasing stream of automated traffic. The gentle 9 mph of the first clumsy coaches now gave way to speed of infinite potential, and Devon was caught fast in the grip of modern tourism.

Now people travelled everywhere by bus or car, paying no heed to the landscape that flashed past. Yet still there remained a few, slower-minded souls who eschewed the growing pace of life, and opted out of society, choosing to make their humble homes wherever nature provided suitable space.

Devon has always had its share of rovers, vagabonds and tramps of both sexes, pushing along the prams or handcarts which carry their few possessions. Lofty and Ginger lived in the woods clothing Telegraph Hill for many years from the 1960s to the early 1980s. Gentle men, they collected sphagnum moss, trundling it into Exeter to sell to florists. The children of Kenn and Kennford knew them well, learning woodland lore from both these knowledgeable and benign wanderers.

Vic, of the fierce mien and crossed-eyes, was a different type. He castigated Chudleigh people throughout the 1960s and 70s when on shopping trips from his 'flat' in a disused limekiln on the top of Haldon. But his shouts of disgust, directed at passing motorists, were gradually accepted and, indeed, sympathised with. Old shirts and trousers, and gifts of food, often came his way, even when he shouted the hardest.

The most famous of all these gentlemen of the road must be Smokey Joe, who set up his patch on the very edge of the A38, almost at the top of Telegraph Hill. He lay full length on the turf, seemingly impassive to the thundering stream of traffic passing within inches of him. But the passers-by were not so impassive, and very soon Joe was famous, his bearded, smoke-browned face, peering from beneath the hood of his disreputable duffle coat, appearing in many a photograph. People stopped to talk to him, gifts and meals were offered, and the media found him extremely newsworthy. Soon Smokey Joe had become a national asset.

His identity remained a mystery, various names coming to light and then being renounced. When, in 1975, he became ill with a liver complaint, he was taken to hospital in Exeter. After treatment, he lived in a guesthouse run by a kindly befriender of social outcasts. He appeared on television, but seeing Joe, all cleaned up and beardless, proved disappointing; the magic had gone. He died a year later, and has never been forgotten, for he was probably the last in a long line of unconforming countryside dwellers, for whom there is no longer space or time.

Today much of Devon is covered with mile after mile of dual carriageway. Even the minor roads are maintained to a state that nomads like Smokey Joe and his forebears would not recognise. But there are still quiet and enchanting rural areas, far from the humming main roads, where the seeker after ancient ways can rediscover old bridleways, green lanes, byways, and forgotten stretches of Roman roads.

Consult a map, ask a local at the nearest village pub to direct you, or just follow your own instinct, and you will be sure to find that green tunnel of a twisting, infuriating, quite magical Devon lane. Drive slowly, or walk expectantly, for these places are still full of the shades of other travellers along the way.

18

Devon Customs

On 5th November every year, the bells of St Michael's church in Shebbear, North Devon, peal out, making a strident, discordant noise.

The purpose is to frighten off any lurking evil spirits, for this is the time of the annual exorcism of the Devil, who once threw down the great boulder lying close to the church, and who now sits there, threatening disaster to the village. In remembrance of this old ritual, and to avoid future repercussions, the Devil's Stone must be turned and its occupier tipped off. On every 5th November, therefore, the bellringers, armed with iron bars, gather around the stone, while the vicar says a prayer; then hefty arms get to grips with the granite and – whew! – Shebbear is safe for another year. Onlookers cheer, the bellringers grin with satisfaction, and pilgrimage is quickly made to the nearby pub – named, of course, the Devil's Stone Inn.

Just another quaint old Devon custom, enjoyed by all, but its history is intriguing. When Christianity came to this Celtic heartland, so deeply immersed in its worship of nature gods and goddesses, no doubt the incoming priests sought to destroy the former pagan worship. No more must the peasantry revere standing stones, springs and wells, old altars – at least, not unless those Celtic holy places were given new dedications to Christian saints, and so considered to contain a new, holier magic.

The Devil's Stone could well have originally been a standing stone, part of those ancient Celtic ceremonies of worship. How easy for the new priest to build a Christian church on the old sacred site, and tell the simple-minded parishioners that their altar was now evil, because possessed by the Devil. Folk memory has retained this ancient belief. Surely, the past is always with us.

A different sort of custom is the old tradition of bee lore. Before sugar became available, the sweetness of the 'bee's gift' was a rare and deeply prized commodity, and its makers thought to be much more than mere insects. Since prehistory, bees have been treated like little gods – loved, feared, and cherished – while the brave men who dared stings, and possibly even more fearsome divine punishment by collecting their honey, were given reverence due to heroes.

Today, science has de-mystified and explained the amazing life of bees, but some of the old lore is charming, and very well worth recalling.

Domestic bees, before their seeming magic was explained in down-to-earth terms, were believed to lead ideal lives. Harmony and industry were the watchwords of each busy hive – or butt, as Devonians called them. Villagers thought that this happy state of life could be reflected into the family home if the bees were kept content. And so, to this end, they were always informed of family news.

This 'telling the bees' emphasised the bond between man and his source of much-desired sweetness. Bees did not thrive in families where there were quarrels and, when told of the death of their master, they had to be reassured that the new master – or mistress – would care for them equally well. If satisfied, the bees would hum to show approval.

After a death in the family, cake and wine would be left beside the hives, carefully saved from the funeral feast, to ensure that the bees would not feel neglected, and so leave home. Various rituals were enacted through the years to prevent such a disaster. In 1790, funeral custom decreed that as the dead master was carried from house to hearse the bee hives must be turned. At Cullompton an ignorant servant unthinkingly turned the hives on their sides. At once the occupants streamed out in an aggressive cloud, stinging everyone in sight. Servants, guests, horsemen and horses ran in dismay, skirts billowing, wigs a-tilt, and voices raised. Meanwhile, the corpse, forgotten, still waited to take its last journey.

Honey was vital to the domestic crafts of preserving, making medicines, polish and candles, generally sweetening food, and, of course, to the all-important process of brewing. Metheglin was a popular, very sweet, drink, made by steeping honeycombs in water and adding various spices. Today it is making a come-back, and metheglin 'kits' are on sale at wine-making centres.

For all these daily gifts, thanks were always given to the ever-generous bees. A good feed of honey and sugar was prepared for the Devon insects on New Year's Day, and on Old Christmas Day, when, according to their owners, who left the yule log and crept near the hives to listen, the bees hummed the Old Hundredth.

Swarming had its own lore, and the bees were said to be 'playing' when this happened. The finder of a swarm of bees following their new queen, 'marked' them and watched until they settled, when he could claim them as his own. Usually he knocked the pulsating, gleaming dark mass into a box, then hurried home to his garden or orchard. But if the swarm clung to a dry branch, then the marker was heading for a speedy death, should he dare take it for himself.

In 1920 Henry Williamson, who told such evocative tales about his life in a North Devon village, wrote about bee-calling in Georgeham. He said he heard a bell being rung one May morning and, going out of his cottage, he found a young girl talking to a neighbour. They were both watching a swarm of bees flying around the tree tops. He called them 'a community in mystic revolution', and was deeply impressed by their strange lifestyle. The girl told him they were playing, and rang her bell to bring them home. Williamson ended his story, 'A dark Assyrian beard began to grow on one of the topmost twigs of the elm. The bees were clustering about the new queen. The girl ceased to shake the hand-bell.'

Before wooden hives were made, bees lived in straw skeps, plaited into cones with arched tops. The occupants came and went through a small entrance at the bottom. In winter the skeps were put into hollowed-out niches in south-facing walls of cottages, farmhouses or barns. In my own home there is a filled-in niche for a skep on the outside wall of the big, old kitchen chimney-breast.

Today, many of our beehives in Devon are deserted, owing to the advent of the vaora mite. Research continues in the hope of finding out how to prevent these predators taking further toll of bees, and anyone who cares enough to grow bee balm and other – mostly blue – bee-attracting flowers in their gardens will still see the industrious, buzzing, silver-winged creatures foraging. Keep the bees happy and you can still earn the mouth-watering reward of 'liquid gold' so revered by our forefathers.

Being a land of rich harvests, Devon has a store of old customs celebrating nature's bounty. Such festivities are thought to stem from pre-Christian times, when it was important to give thanks to the appropriate pagan deities who made such gifts possible, and to woo them into continuing the practice.

The corn harvest was probably the most important occasion for celebration in the pastoral year, but Devon's farmers – and their thirsty labourers – also made a point of thanking the god of the apple trees for giving them the fruit which made rough cider, or scrumpy, as it is called in Devon. Made from fermented apple juice, this was the working man's standard thirst-quencher. Most farm labourers carried cider jars with their snack meals of bread, cheese and raw onion during the long working day. These stone containers were known as badgers, and it was a welcome break when the farmer said, 'tis time to kiss the badger, boys.'

Physical labour, in the years before machinery was used, made men sweat copiously, and it was vital to drink deeply in order to avoid dehydration. So it behoved all cider-drinkers to make the annual pilgrimage of thanks and entreaty to the old god perched up there above the apple orchard. It was a ceremony called 'wassailing the apple trees', and originally took place on the eve of Twelfth Night. This date is an indication of ancient origin, from before the calendar changed in 1752. Now wassailing is celebrated on the 16th January, the eve of the twelfth night after 5th January, Old Christmas Day.

The word wassailing comes from the Anglo-Saxon 'woes hal', thought to mean 'be thou of good health'. The ceremony began with farmers, their families and labourers, going into the orchard at night, choosing the most fruitful tree, be it Tom Putt, Bloody

Butcher, Queenie, Slack-Ma-Girdle, Fair Maid of Devon, or any other old-time favourite, and making rough music – that is, beating pans and irons to drive away any evil spirits lurking with intent to harm the tree. Once firearms were common in every farmhouse, guns were shot instead, and even as recently as 1936 we read that a salvo was heard in an apple orchard in Topsham, in South Devon. A bowl of cider would then be poured over the roots of the tree, with pieces of toast, which had been floating in the dish, placed upon the branches. Sometimes a small boy climbed into the tree to accept the oblation, presumably enacting the part of the god himself. While the votive offering was being made, the wassailers sang a lusty hymn of praise.

> 'Here's to thee, old apple tree,
> Whence thou may'st bud, and whence thou may'st blow!
> And whence thou may'st bear apples enow!
> Hats full! Caps full!
> Bushel, bushel, sacks full!
> And my pockets full too! Huzza!'

The regenerating spirit of green thought running through the countryside today has revived this old custom in many West Country villages. Whether the rituals are still carried out in deference to ancient deities is in doubt, but the same spirit of joy seems very much in evidence.

Customs and habits die hard, as Theo Brown, the late Devon folklorist relates. Visiting a man in the Teign valley who, for the last 30 years had taken his gun, every Twelfth Night, and fired it into the tops of his apple trees and said he always had a good crop of fruit, she asked if it was an old family custom.

'No', said the man. 'I 'eerd a chap on the wireless say as it were the thing to do.'

19

The Prayer Book Rebellion

Father Harper looked at his sunlit church in the small, serene village of Sampford Courtenay, and sighed as he prepared for the morning service. Whit Sunday, 9th June 1549 – the deadline set by the government for the introduction of the new prayer book, and the establishment of the unwanted Protestant faith.

The priest knew trouble lay ahead. The sleepy little village was rapidly filling with his church-going flock, and already feelings were running high. Farm labourers and their families, arriving on foot and in carts and wagons, were all here to see how he would deal with the extraordinary situation.

Father Harper himself sympathised with his parishioners, knowing that the familiar Catholic Mass, delivered in Latin, together with the rituals and adornments of the service, were a source of comfort and beauty to men who worked long hours for little pay, and to the women who strove to keep families surviving on breadline wages. Somehow they lived on milk, cheese, curds and butter. They were barefoot, their clothes and dwellings of the shabbiest. Hard lives, indeed. For the promises of old King Harry, who had initially brought about this change in religion, of better wages and lower rents, had never materialised. No wonder the priest, looking about him, saw surly faces and more than a hint of defiance.

And then there were the agitators. Their loud voices proclaimed to the listening, gullible peasantry exactly how they had been duped. How the new faith, with its subsequent growing gap between landowners and tenants, must inevitably hang a

further burden about necks already bowed by rising rents and the menace of starvation. Without doubt, rebellion was in the air. 'Rise up, brothers – if there are enough of us protesting we can keep things as we want them! Stand up for your rights!'

It only needed a small spark to fire the inflamed passions, thought Father Harper wretchedly, and there would be an ugly explosion of violence.

He appeared in church without his usual Catholic vestments and heard the parishioners gasp, but the new Protestant service took place without incident, although afterwards, outside, once again the shouts and the arguments arose. But because the next day was the annual ale festival, the men agreed to disperse and meet again on Whit Monday morning.

Monday found the agitators there in louder, more persuasive voice. The crowd, swayed by their manipulation, hectored poor

Father Harper to return to the old faith, which, reluctantly, he did. After celebrating the Mass, his act of downright rebellion ran like wildfire through the countryside, bringing the local magistrates into the village, trying to calm the men by showing them the stupidity of what they were trying to do. Tempers, already high, flared. The crowd pushed forward. Someone jostled one of the magistrates, and the man fell. . .

This was the spark Father Harper had feared. It ignited instantly. A farmer armed with a billhook struck at the fallen man, and was joined by others. The magistrate, William Hellyons, was cut into pieces.

Now fully committed to rebellion, the crowd began marching to Exeter. At Crediton they met with insurgents from Cornwall, who had also risen in defiance of the new faith. For the Cornish, many of whom spoke only Celtic, the introduction of a service in

English must have been unthinkable. Now they were here in their thousands, armed with whatever weapons they could find – billhooks, staves, clubs and knives – resolved to besiege Exeter and force the issue.

The Government in London, already harried by impending wars with France and negotiations with Scotland, hoped to put an end to the small West Country rising before it got out of hand. With no forces to spare, they sent two soldier-courtiers to Devon in the hope of sweet-talking the rebels into dispersing. 'Tell them that their complaints will be considered by the Privy Council: above all, tell them to go home.'

Sir Peter and Sir Gawen Carew rode fast, changing horses constantly, only to find when they reached Exeter that the rebels were encamped at Crediton. The Carews rode out to confer with the leaders, but the bridge at the Exeter end of the town was blocked, and the rebels entrenched in the two barns that bordered the road. There was instant refusal to confer. Anger and sudden violence resulted in the barns being fired. Humiliated by their inability to accomplish their mission, the firmly committed Protestant Carews rode back to Exeter, with the united Catholic army following them.

What a spectacle of sight and sound. Robed priests, clouds of incense, sacred banners of the Five Holy Wounds of Christ flying in the breeze, chanting and singing filling the air, and, amongst it all, a feeling of resolute aggression. It was a rough, homespun little army of Devon and Cornish farmers and labourers, led by a few members of West Country gentry. But, small and ill-armed as it undoubtedly was, it made clear the rebels' determination to do all they could to maintain the old solid comfort of their hard lives – their old-established Catholic religion. As they marched, others joined them. Soon the whole countryside was in turmoil. On Tuesday, 2nd July, despite the mayor's Catholic sympathies, Exeter shut its five gates, and a siege commenced which was to last five weeks.

During this time, many incidents have been recorded in old books. Walls were scaled and mined, gates burned. Spies passed messages and Catholic supporters inside the city deviously plotted to sabotage the defences. The rebels caught and hanged a man slipping out to carry a letter to a king's officer, an act which was to have later repercussions.

By now, the Government had at last realised the seriousness of the situation and despatched Lord John Russell, an avid Protestant thinker and, as a newly enriched landowner, through the late King Henry's sales of dispossessed monastic land, clearly a most unsuitable person to work out terms with the rebels.

Delays in raising money and men hindered him initially, but finally, with an army of German and Italian mercenaries, Russell rode down into the West Country. The rebels, alerted to his arrival, decided to attack, and confronted the king's army at Fenny Bridges, two miles from Honiton. There was no bridge in those days, only a ford bordered by tranquil watermeadows. The battle of Fenny Meadows, as it became known, made the river run blood, and ended in crushing defeat for the West Country men. Although the Cornish and Devon forces fought with immense passion and bravery, they were no match for the heavily armed mercenaries.

This decisive campaign was followed by a battle on Clyst Heath within a few days, as a result of which the little village of Clyst St Mary was fired and all the villagers were put to the sword. Lord Russell followed up this brutality by ordering the slaughter of all prisoners taken. His mercenaries are said to have killed 900 men in ten minutes.

With the withdrawal of the rebels, Exeter was relieved, and there followed all the revenges and repercussions which could only be expected. Russell set up gallows everywhere and the corpses of the wrongdoers swung in villages throughout the West Country. Particularly horrific was the hanging of the vicar of St Thomas, outside Exeter's city gate, who had done the besieged citizens a good turn by preventing a rebel from setting fire to the town with red-hot shot. Russell excused his action by contending it was only retaliation for the hanging of his messenger, carried out by the rebels at the start of the siege. He erected a gibbet on the tower of the church in St Thomas, and, as we are told by a writer some 50 years after the event, Father Robert Welsh was '. . . there in chains hanged in his popish apparel and having a holy water bucket, a sprinkle, a sacring bell, a pair of beads and such other popish trash hanged about him.' What a vivid image his seemingly casual description evokes, especially as we know that Father Welsh's remains hung from that church-top gibbet for many years.

Such acts of revenge and brutality have always been the aftermath of wars and uprisings, and in those troubled times punishment was barbaric. The leaders of the rebellions were finally caught, taken to London, and executed in the customary manner of hanging, drawing and quartering.

But, before the rebellion could truly be called over, a last stand was made in the village where it began – Sampford Courtenay. The remnants of the rebel army entrenched themselves there, stretching a great plough chain across the road to deter Russell's pursuing cavalry. To no avail. The pursuit continued, as did the subsequent slaughter and imprisonments. The 710 killed and 700 prisoners taken, we are told, finally wiped out the army of Cornish and Devon men who had stood up so passionately and stubbornly for what they believed in.

Today, at least in England, religious toleration is the norm and it is hard to understand the discord and fury that the first prayer book of Edward VI engendered. Visiting the peaceful village centre of Sampford Courtenay, violence and hatred seem long gone. The church of St Thomas stands now in the middle of a busy Exeter suburb, and Blood Meadow – Fenny Meadow's previous name – has come down through the centuries as a vague memory of a half-forgotten battle, its cause no longer important.

Yet it is not entirely forgotten, for local folklore, with its undying power of retrospection, insists that anyone standing on Fenny Bridge on a moonlit night 'will see horsemen plunging about the meadows, up to their hocks in blood.'

20

Sir Francis Drake and the Devil

Explorer, adventurer, merchant, preacher, public benefactor, hero and pirate – Sir Francis Drake was all of these. Adored as he was by his fellow countrymen, favoured by his queen and feared by the mighty Spaniards, there was always a sense of wonder at the undoubted power that he possessed. It was probably this very awe, heightened perhaps by natural envy, that induced a darker thread into the amazing stories that grew around him.

In the Tudor age, when belief in the supernatural was very real, it must have seemed quite logical to ally such charisma and extravagant prowess to that well-known and respected helpmate, the Devil. For, as every recently converted good Protestant citizen knew, the Devil was alive and well in England, always looking for a chance to harass the Church, as it proceeded on its controversial and powerful way.

They argued – how did such a man, a stocky young Devonian, with a thick accent and poor background, rise to the heights that Drake achieved? It all seemed very sinister. Against the heaviest odds of capricious winds, pestilential fevers aboard small ships – not to mention the heavily armed force of the Spanish Colonies – time and again he sailed home triumphant from his voyages, with his little fleet of 'diminutive men-of-war' piled high with booty. Precious metals, rare spices and treasure, both coin and jewels, all helped fill the queen's coffers. She fondly called Drake her 'pirate', willingly investing in yet another voyage with its ensuing raids on Spanish trading routes and ports. Slowly but surely it became obvious to the incredulous peasantry, as Drake capped one amazing deed with the next, that the Devil must be helping him out.

When he returned safely home from his three year circum-navigation of the globe, which opened up a new seaway for the world, Drake settled into a new home with Mary, his wife, and the gossips got busy again. Drake had bought Buckland Abbey from the famous Grenville family, who had turned it into a house after the Dissolution, before which it had been a Cistercian abbey. These were the facts, but folklore has infinite licence and facts can be pulled one way or the other. How much more convenient – and exciting – to tell one's neighbours that without doubt it was the Devil who had enabled Drake to live in such a once-holy place. The Devil getting his own back on the monks who once prayed there.

Elected as Mayor of Plymouth, Drake sought to improve conditions in his native city. He instigated a scheme for bringing a supply of fresh water down from Dartmoor. But, again, it was said to be with Devilish aid. Drake cast a spell on a moorland stream, went the story, and the sparkling water then ran behind him as he rode back into Plymouth. This particular bit of embroidery, however, has a hitch in it, as the project actually took ten years to complete.

Drake's wife died within a few years of moving into Buckland, and it wasn't long before he chose another bride. And here a very strange tale sprang into being.

Elizabeth Sydenham was tall, beautiful, and half her famous suitor's age. Small wonder that her aristocratic parents did not approve of a middle-aged husband, from humble origins, who could not be relied upon to stay at home and conduct a normal married life. They warned Elizabeth about having to live, as Mary had done, alone, and with the constant shadow of fear of losing her sailor husband to the merciless sea that called him so urgently and so constantly. But love defied the parental warning, and Elizabeth married Francis in 1585 at Monksilver church, close to her family home in Coombe Sydenham, on Exmoor. She stayed on there after the marriage, awaiting Drake's return from the next long sea voyage. Nothing was heard of him for several years. Elizabeth pondered on her parents' advice. Then rumour whispered that Drake had perished at sea. Quickly, the parents told Elizabeth she must consider herself a widow. The law of the land confirmed her ability to remarry after seven years, even without the certainty of her husband's death. Pressing home their point, the parents persuaded unhappy Elizabeth to consider marriage with her previous suitor, who was far more likely to make her a good husband.

Elizabeth dithered, but finally gave in. Yet her heart kept telling her Drake was still alive. She prayed desperately for some sort of sign to guide her, so that she might avoid a bigamous re-marriage. On the day of the wedding, she came downstairs from her chamber, followed by her maids who had helped dress her in bridal finery. Guests, family and her new groom waited in the hall. The young man came forward, taking her hand, and then – a blinding flash, a roar like thunder, and a huge round object hurtled into the house, parting Elizabeth and her husband-to-be. Elizabeth's reaction was ecstatic. 'Drake is alive and I am still a wife.'

Drake was, indeed, in Plymouth. He arrived next day and took Elizabeth away from Coombe Sydenham – but left the famous cannonball. It remained in the old house for centuries, and became a fascinating reminder of Drake's rumoured alliance with supernatural forces. The fact that contemporary experts have identified the object as a meteorite has made no difference to the lore surrounding its amazing arrival.

When Drake, in 1588, sailed from Plymouth to meet the mighty two-horned crescent of the Spanish Armada, it was firmly believed that the Devil stood at his elbow, on his man-of-war, blowing the wind which first turned the Spanish ships, sending them drifting in the wrong direction, and then kindling the fireships, with which the English – with Drake as second-in-command – finally destroyed the Spanish fleet.

Drake's story is set in a time when England was restless and seeking new dominions, new adventures. He was a true Renaissance man, and will always be remembered for his achievements with which he brought excitement and glory to his country. Perhaps the most long-lived facet of the folklore that has grown around him is the magic of his famous drum. Smart and newly made for his journey around the globe, it was always to be heard prior to his ship going into action. In attacks on Spanish settlements, he advanced towards the enemy with a trumpet blaring, and the drum beating a noisy tattoo. When he was knighted by the queen, Drake proudly had his drum painted with his new coat of arms, celebrating his rise from a humble background. It was used on board at musters and ceremonies.

When Drake, in 1596, realised he was dying from dysentery – 'the bludy flix' he called it – he summoned his servant to his cabin and ordered that he should be dressed in full armour, ready for death and ensuing rituals. As his coffin slipped overboard, into Nombre de Dios Bay, the drum's crackling beat counterpointed the mournful wail of the trumpets.

Drake's drum remains the centrepiece of his legendary fame today. Called 'England's beating heart', the story of the drum is far more seriously considered than the other tales folklore recounts. Drake himself said he would return from the grave if England was ever in danger. When he heard his drum, he would be there, all his ingenuity, strength and courage at his beloved country's disposal yet again.

This legend is insistent. Now in the National Trust's safe-keeping at Buckland Abbey, Drake's drum has been heard to beat on various occasions in the not-so-distant past.

It sounded when Napoleon was brought into Plymouth Sound as a prisoner on the *Bellerophon*; when Nelson was made a Freeman of the Borough; and at the start of the Second World War, when its ghostly, pulsing tattoo was said to beat on Plymouth Hoe.

Today, looking at Drake's formidable statue on the Hoe, and recalling the amazing vitality and achievement of the man, the legend of his drum has an inspiring quality. But as to whose is the master-hand, wielding the drumsticks in time of need, no answer can be given. Like most folklore, the truth is veiled by centuries of gossip, inaccuracy, exaggeration, and – above all – personal imagination.

21

All the Fun of the Fair

'Roll up! Roll up! Here are bargains. . .' Through the centuries hawkers and traders have shouted their wares in this way at markets and fairs, and they still do. Before history recorded the first grants of charters, enabling markets and fairs to be held, our early ancestors drove their caravans of sheep and cattle, or silver, tin and lead, to the nearest mutually convenient meeting point. There they haggled and bartered and gossiped before celebrating with the local brew.

Such meeting places were often at the junction of green lanes, drove roads and old tracks, at boundary stones or at hilltop camps. Great social occasions for scattered communities, as well as trade gatherings, fairs often developed into licentious firelit orgies, and so it's not surprising that by the 12th century, the Crown had regularised these wild events. It was decreed then that fairs and markets could only be held where a charter had been granted.

Usually, the grant of a charter was made to a noble landowner in reward for services rendered to the Crown, or, if the landowner was a religious establishment, as an endowment to help with the upkeep of that particular abbey or priory. In effect, the charter meant that the Crown gathered revenue from the landowner, who in turn levied tolls on the traders attending the fair. Fairs were the most important means of trading in times when population was scattered and transport difficult.

They generally opened with a ceremony. The charter was read aloud, and sometimes a glove, or a model of a hand, was hoisted aloft on a pole. This was a sign of the sovereign's pledge to protect all comers honestly and in accord with the terms of charter. In some fairs and markets the glove is still raised.

The three-day Michaelmas fair held at the prehistoric campsite just below Brentor, on the western side of Dartmoor, is believed to have been held 'under the sign of the glove', but presumably even that regal symbol was not strong enough to stop the roistering and disorders that went on, once the hippocras started flowing. As a result, the fair's venue was moved to Tavistock in the middle of the 16th century – the precedent of today's Goose Fair.

No fair was ever complete without its cheapjacks. These travelling hawkers were relied upon by the local countryfolk to arrive with carts full of useful bargains. Such goods were bought from manufactories in far away towns at enormous discounts and then sold quickly for hard cash. Then, as now, turnover was what mattered, and such traders were highly skilled in their methods of ensuring a speedy return on their outlay. Just the raucous shout of 'roll up, roll up' was enough to pull a crowd. Then, quickfire chatter, the rattling off of bawdy jokes and, above all, an entertaining patter would always ensure sales. The experienced cheapjack cultivated a loud voice, and the knack of being thought of as 'one of us'.

Often it was necessary to show his power. Famous Harry Perdue, who frequented Barnstaple's fair in the 1830s, was renowned for his aggression. On one occasion, he grabbed hold of his assistant, who had foolishly undersold an item, taking him by his collar and the seat of his pants, and threw him over the heads of the surrounding crowd. And then, amid the suddenly respectful silence, he continued with the sales patter.

We still have cheapjacks at local markets today, plausible and vastly entertaining characters who are able to draw a big audience around their stalls. Most customers merely go to enjoy the performance, but by the end are almost hypnotised into buying. For who can resist the seductive build-up of falling prices?

'Not five pounds, not four, not three – ladies and gents, not even two. . .' A long pause, while everybody holds their breath in anticipation. 'But – and this is my final offer, my friends! I'm giving you the opportunity of buying this beautiful towel/pair of sheets/china tea set/pirated video/teddy bear made in Taiwan – did I say buying? Ladies and gents, I'm GIVING it away! Now, here

we go – not two pounds, not even one, but. . .' The voice rises to a practised crescendo of intensity. '. . .but FIFTYPENCE!' And the money comes in so fast he can hardly handle it. What a performance.

At Newton Abbot's annual Cheese and Onion Fair, held in early September, there are many attractions. A procession, headed by the Town Crier, resplendent in cocked hat and elegant costume, is followed by the mayoral retinue, all escorted by a raggle-taggle assortment of drummers and pikeman, recruited from the local English Civil War Society. In the market precinct, the great brass bell clangs three times before a stentorian 'Oyez!' is proclaimed, after which the charter is read. And then it's time for all the fun of the fair. Rides on carousels and dodgems in the nearby fairground, the cheese tasting, the onion buying, the judging of costumed stallholders competing for the annual prize. And, in between doing the rounds of the various crowded tables and stalls, there's time to pause for a cup of coffee, while watching the juggler busy with his seven oranges, and the unicyclist, always on the verge of falling off his wobbling wheel. And perhaps, also, time to remember the origin of this particular market, when cheese and onions were the staple diet of the peasantry, and Somerset cheesemakers travelled the dusty roads to come to what was then Newton Bushell to sell their wares, and to join in the jollifications.

Fairs and markets have always been a vital part of Devon's economy, but nowadays most of the old, traditional fairs have become places of amusement, with sales of livestock channelled into different venues, and at different times.

Barnstaple and Widecombe-in-the-Moor, both important fairs in the past, have now grown into the rollicking day-out entertainment associated with stalls and sideshows – and teeming crowds.

Tavistock's population is said to expand enormously when the Goose Fair takes place on the second Wednesday in October each year. No geese are driven to the fair today, grazing on stubble fields as they once did; sales of fat geese were many tenants' only hope of finding the rent money traditionally due to the landlord on St Michael's Day. But the fair continues on its merry way, despite annual threats of imminent closure. Public demand for this last high-spot of the rural year before winter sets in remains insistent. Indeed, so popular is the Goose Fair that market traders and entertainers from all around the country come to Tavistock, setting up their stalls throughout the town, and filling usually quiet spaces with noisy shooting galleries, dodgems, ghost trains and the rest of the amusements calculated to fill the populace with joy. And if the day is noisy, the evening is chaotic, with brilliant lights, and the beat of tannoyed music throbbing out into the surrounding dark countryside.

And the geese? Alas, the one remaining link with the origin of this festive day is the goose lunches served in the town's cafés and restaurants. Times change. But the hope continues that future years will still hear the echo of the famous old song, with its refrain entreating one and all 'to stap down long ter Tavistock Goozey Vair!'

22

Fathers and Mothers in a Strange Land

Jacques Fontaine stared anxiously through the blustering, salt-whipped darkness, trying to make out the shape of the ship on which he had booked passage for himself and his band of fellow-fugitives. The sea heaved and slapped at the creaking timbers, as the little fishing boat bore them secretly out of the French port of La Rochelle towards the English ship, the *Industry*, bound for far-away Barnstaple in North Devon, port of its origin and their hoped-for place of asylum.

John Dennis, master of the *Industry*, had agreed to this awkward subterfuge of allowing his passengers to board at sea, because he knew of the French authority's ban on refugees leaving La Rochelle. It was 1685 and the very height of the persecution of the French Protestants, the Huguenots. Dennis knew also that he could demand high passage money from his helpless passengers, but at least he was an honest man, and not one of the many other sea captains who duped terrified fugitives by taking their money and then either leaving them ashore or, worse, drowning them. John Dennis was willing to give what help he could to Fontaine's party.

Huddled together in the small, heaving boat and at last in sight of the *Industry*, Fontaine's heart sank as he saw a French frigate approaching. It could only mean that the authorities had ordered searches of all foreign vessels leaving harbour. What if they were found and so lost all hope of freedom? And even if they were not discovered, would the English master think the project too dangerous and abandon them as a result?

Jacques Fontaine thought hard. He evolved a plan – a risky one, but something had to be done, and fast. Somehow he persuaded the crew of the fishing boat to hide him and his party. And, as the frigate drew closer, he asked the fishermen to pretend to be drunk. Obligingly, they swayed and grinned stupidly, at the same time lowering the sails three times, the pre-arranged signal to the English vessel to take them aboard.

It worked. Seeing an obviously drunken crew, not even able to control its own sails, the men on the frigate shouted contemptuous insults and then moved off in search of more likely prey. And so Jacques, his fiancée Mademoiselle Elizabeth-Anne Boursiquot, his young sister, four other young women and two men, boarded the *Industry* safely and so began their eleven day voyage to England.

Overcrowded, seasick, afraid, and without sufficient provisions or weatherproof clothing, they arrived at Appledore on Sunday, 1st December, sailing on up the estuary of the river Taw to the *Industry*'s home port of Barnstaple, where they disembarked and stood shivering on the quayside, a distressed, vulnerable group, wondering what to do next.

But, despite Jacques' near-penniless state, his faith was great. He firmly believed that he and his friends would find refuge in England. He told the others that God had not brought them safely as far as Barnstaple only to let them die now. Bravely, they walked up towards the market square and there, as if in answer to his words, the good folk of Barnstaple, emerging from divine service, came to look at the fugitives cast up on their shore, and acted with great kindness and generosity. Perhaps they had heard tales of the savage laws brought into being in France against the Protestants – how ministers were threatened with exile or the galleys. And how only their wives, and children of under 7 years, could accompany them, if their choice was exile. Whatever the reason, hearts and homes were instantly opened, and in ones and twos the refugees were invited into merchants' houses, peasant cottages, inns and shops, to be dried, warmed, fed – and reassured.

Mademoiselle Boursiquot was taken in by the Fraine family, who were rich merchants, as were Mr and Miss Downe who offered hospitality to Jacques Fontaine.

There must have been many fascinating anecdotes and happenings arisings from this Huguenot emigration and the Barnstaple citizens' reactions to them. Certainly, Jacques Fontaine's experience is worth the telling. In due course, having settled in with Joseph Downe and his unmarried sister, Jacques discovered, with alarm, that Miss Downe had taken a fancy to him.

In his memoirs, almost as if to reassure himself about his engagement, he lists the attractions of his intended, the beautiful Mademoiselle Boursiquot. Indeed, he rhapsodises – 'skin delicately fair, brilliant colour in cheeks, high forehead, remarkably intellectual expression of countenance, her bust was fine, rather inclined to embonpoint, and she had a very dignified courage, which some people condemned as haughty, but I – thought peculiarly becoming to her beauty.'

Miss Downe, he remarks bluntly, was short and thin, sallow of complexion and spotted by the smallpox. So it's not surprising that when she made the forthright suggestion that he would be better advised to marry her and thus make use of her fortune, while her brother would look after Miss Boursiquot, Jacques said a very firm no, thank you. But the mere idea that his beloved fiancée might, indeed, prefer to be cared for by wealthy Mr Downe caused him to call at once upon her, offering to renounce his claim, if that was what she wished. It must have resulted in a highly emotional scene, with mutual understanding causing great woe.

Jacques tells us, 'she burst into tears, thinking I wished to break off our engagement, attracted by Miss Downe's fortune.'

'You are free, I release you. . .' Mademoiselle Boursiquot's sobs finally allowed her to add that she would never marry another.

'It was too much for me,' confessed Jacques. 'My turn to weep and our tears flowed together. . .'

Finally, of course, all was made clear and she agreed to marry him, but still honest Jacques had to warn her. 'Remember, poverty is a hard, grinding mistress, and one under whom we shall be obliged to work hard all the days of our lives.'

But his loving fiancée reassured him. 'Every word you say finds its answering echo in my breast.'

They were married on 8th February 1686, at the parish church in Barnstaple. Both Mr Downe and the Fraines gave generous wedding feasts, to which most of the French community in the neighbourhood were invited. Miss Downe, however, was not pleased with the outcome of the affair, and we are not told of her behaviour at the jollifications.

The Fontaines lived in a furnished room for a month or two, until some bedding was sent from Jacques' previous home in France. His sister sent household linen from London and, thus equipped, the newly married couple moved into a small house. The Barnstaple folk, quite caught up in this tale of true love, gave small gifts, until the household was made comfortable. On market days anonymous presents of meat, corn and vegetables were left at the door. Eventually, the Fontaines moved away. In Taunton they opened a shop, prospered and had six children before moving again, this time to Ireland, where Jacques eventually took holy orders and lived to a good age.

Always aware of the help he and his fellow refugees had encountered upon their arrival in Devon, he wrote gratefully in his memoirs, 'The good people of Barnstaple were full of compassion, they took us into their houses and treated us with the greatest kindness. Thus God raised up for us Fathers and Mothers in a Strange Land.'

But it was not only words that expressed the gratitude of the Huguenot refugees, for, as they settled and slowly became part of the life of the town, their various crafts and skills, as well as their contacts, with Europe, did much to help Barnstaple to enlarge its trade and develop into a more prosperous town.

The old French names have weathered the centuries, emerging here and there in slightly more Devonian editions. Roch, for instance, became Rock; L'Oiseau, Bird; and the beautiful, if haughty, Elizabeth-Anne Boursiquot's name has been simplified into the more homely Bursicott.

Barnstaple today, if you care to look, is full of echoes of those busy times of immigrant arrivals. You only have to watch the powerful river Taw slapping the grey stone quay where the *Industry* moored and you can visualise the fugitives' first hesitant steps into a seemingly empty and alien town, and evoke the confrontation, in the town centre, of travel-weary foreigners and astonished Barnstaple citizens, as they made their way home to Sunday dinner.

Once established in their new homes, the Huguenot community were allowed to hold their own Sunday services in St Anne's Chapel – now a museum – despite its everyday usage as the local school. The list of crafts the Huguenots brought to the town is long and various. They were gold and silversmiths, dyers, soap-boilers, woollen and silk weavers, carpet makers, hatters and haberdashers, potters and clockmakers. And many other trades, as well. Besides spreading their talents around Devon, some of the new settlers married into wealthy local families and became celebrated citizens of the towns that had befriended them. Mathew Roch served twice as Mayor of Barnstaple in the 18th century.

All in all, it seems that this 'Quiet Conquest', as it has been aptly named, has more than repaid the open-hearted welcome offered by the good citizens of Barnstaple, some three centuries ago.

23

Charms, Curses and Incantations

The girl and the child watched the old woman, Hannah Henley, shuffle up the lane towards them, and the girl instinctively put her hand on the boy's shoulder. But he was too quick for her. He ran towards Hannah, offering her the nut he was playing with. Horror stricken, the girl also ran, snatching him away. But the harm was done. Hannah bent and drew a circle in the dust of the lane. She added a cross to the circle. The child died four days later.

Of course, said the village, we always knew Hannah was a witch; a shape-changer, too. Didn't she turn herself into a hare and escape the local harriers? She's a proper nuisance. Don't go near her. Don't give her anything.

When Hannah turned up at the farm belonging to the dead child's father, he turned her away immediately, refusing her plea for money. Even her warning didn't sway him – 'You won't live long enough to enjoy your money, Maister.' Now the whole family was terrorised. Horses, cows and lambs died on the farm, and indoors the bread refused to rise. The farmer's wife was glued to the steps outside the house when Hannah again came, asking for money, and her outraged husband, reaching for his gun, could not pull the trigger.

More deaths occurred among the farm stock, and eventually the distraught farmer consulted a Wise Man from a neighbouring village. Rituals and spells were concocted and, after hanging six bullocks' hearts, pierced with thorns, in the fireplace, the Wise Man confessed that getting rid of Hannah was proving his most testing case. But his magic worked. As the hearts rotted, so Hannah was seen to grow frailer and more desperate. She crawled to the farmhouse again, begging for food and help. Neither was given, and she died. A hundred pounds – a very large sum in those days – passed hands, and the satisfied Wise Man returned to his own home.

This terrifying story is engrained in East Devon folklore, but when research was carried out as to factual evidence, quite a different tale emerged.

It appears that 80 year old Hannah Henley, of Membury village near Axminster, died mysteriously in 1841. Two inquests were held and the case was given much publicity in the local press. Frail and alone in the world, she had lived with three cats on two shillings a week, plus a loaf of bread. She was last seen by some huntsmen, when she asked them to help her to lift her bundle of sticks over a gate. Because of her reputation no one would do so. Found dying two days later by concerned village women, she warned them to leave her alone as her death was going to be a hard one. The next day she was discovered dead outside her cottage. Folklore interrupts here to insist that she dangled on a tree, which had to be cut down to reach her, but the inquest reported her as having fallen in the stream outside her cottage, where she had gone to fill her kettle.

An autopsy showed brain damage, probably causing her strange behaviour. She died of apoplexy and was buried in an unmarked grave. Again, folklore has a different version, relating that she was buried at a cross between two parishes, the stream running between both and neither wanting the responsibility of owning her. As loud voices were said to have been heard in her cottage after her death, the inquisitive villagers entered to see what they could find. There was a box of toads – certain proof of witchcraft – by her bed. The three cats escaped all efforts to catch them, and finally the cottage was burned down. No sign of it now remains, although 'the witch's grave' is talked about still.

A thought-provoking pair of stories – but which version can be believed? The folklore of witchcraft overflows with equally horrifying and fascinating tales, about which time has slowly hung a hazy veil. Perhaps the only certain thing is that such men and women really did exist, and still do.

Undoubtedly people of great power, they were called Wise Men and Women, Enchanters, Sorcerers and Conjurors in past centuries. Well-versed in a variety of rural crafts, which naturally set them apart from the primitive, unlearned communities in which they lived, they were 'different', and so instantly condemned. Knowing which herbal remedies worked on which symptoms, having a snippet of amateur veterinarian knowledge, and, most important of all, possessing absolute faith in their own abilities to work 'magic', were the main components of these old healers' armouries.

Their wisdom, used in a benevolent way, was of immense value to neighbouring farms and homesteads. With a Wise Woman's aid, many a sick animal recovered. Many a barren, desperate wife eventually conceived – or, conversely, a fecund one was helped to put an end to the wearisome annual pregnancy. Countless were the other small, but blessed advantages of having a Cunning Man or Woman in the neighbourhood, to be called upon in times of need. Warts and ringworm were charmed away, bleeding wounds staunched by a muttered incantation, and often a lovesick maiden, given a love potion, persuaded the man she loved to pop the question.

Never did the healer or charmer ask for payment, for they believed the gift would leave them if rewarded. Which must leave some doubt over the hundred pounds said to have been paid in the Hannah Henley case.

The powers of healing, cursing, scrying and over-looking were handed down through the generations, and always between the sexes. Should there be no one thought worthy of receiving the gift, it was allowed to die with its current owner.

The wild terrain of Devon – particularly on Dartmoor and Exmoor – is particularly rich in tales of these strange, talented, dangerous people, for the remote and enclosed communities in which they lived had implicit faith in the supernatural. White witches were respected, but grey witches, who could overlook and cause harm, and particularly black witches, with their reputation

of malevolent evil, were kept at a distance. At the slightest hint of something out of the ordinary happening in the village, suspicion grew fast, within the hotbed of fireside and farmyard gossip.

Like Hannah, at Membury, the local Wise Woman was often just a lonely old person, living with her dog or cat. She was seen collecting herbs, gathering firewood and watching her neighbours. If she also had a way with animals, then curiosity gave way to fear. And if, sometimes, she used the control of her focused mind to stop anyone annoying her – hostile beast, man, or rascally child – then people forgot she was old and vulnerable and said of course she had the Evil Eye. After that she was talked about, dreaded and, when a safe opportunity arose, accused and punished. 'Swimming' witches in the local pond or river was the popular way of discovering their guilt. If the accused sank, she was innocent. If she swam, her guilt was proven.

But most Wise Men and Women avoided retribution, for they had the sensitivity to see it coming. Watching their neighbours was one of the great sources for their prophecies, and the accrued knowledge could name the likely thief in the village, or the scarlet woman who visited the woods after dark to meet her lover. Such basic psychology also enabled the healer to give, as well as charms and spells, the words of common sense needed to help untangle the twisted threads of life that were often presented to them, following a secret knocking at the door. Wise folk, indeed.

So it seems that the wisdom of these people wasn't all 'magic', as their hostile neighbours believed. But, even so, some of the stories handed down from the past – and even in our present century – cannot so easily be explained away.

A tale is told in Countisbury, on Exmoor in North Devon, of a white witch being tested for proof of her power, and found genuine. The landlord of the Blue Ball Inn drove a wooden peg through the woman's footprint, embedded in the clay of the churchyard one Sunday. On her knees in church she was seen to be unable to rise until he withdrew the peg.

Mrs Bray, an avid documenter of folklore in the mid-19th century, told of various charms she had learned from local healers around Tavistock, where she lived.

A charm for a scald or burn, with the charmer putting her hand on the wound, was:

'Three angels came from the North, East and West.
One brought fire, another brought Ice.
And the third brought the Holy Ghost.
So out fire, in frost.
In the name of the Father, Son and Holy Ghost, Amen.'

Such incantations, and there are many of them recorded over the years, are an obvious mix of words from the Bible added to the mumbo-jumbo of illiterate minds.

Theo Brown, the late folklorist of Devon, wrote of the white witch of Dartmoor, Mrs Webb, the most famous of all healers. Mrs Webb, living in Postbridge and dying in 1913, was a charmer of warts which she 'struck' with a peeled reed. But her special talent was to stop bleeding, which she did merely by telling the messenger who came running for help to return to the patient, for the bleeding had already stopped. And it had.

Healers and charmers still practised on Dartmoor in the middle of the 20th century, to Theo Brown's knowledge. She declined to name names, insisting that their privacy should be respected. Perhaps this is why one seldom hears of Wise Men and Women today. Yet they still exist, in various places, living out their private, gifted and often helpful lives as they have always done.

A friend told me of her encounter with a local Wise Woman. 'To cure a wart on my horse,' she said, 'I was told to go to his field at midnight when there was a full moon. I was to take a hair from his tail and wrap this around the wart, at the same time reciting three times – "In the name of the Lord, I viggy viggy thee." ' My friend said she did all this, but added that she tried it during daylight, not having the courage to visit the horse at midnight under a full moon. It would be satisfying to say that the charm worked; alas, it failed. The horse was taken to a vet who burned off the wart. Plainly, the magic couldn't work because all the conditions had not been complied with.

But here is an example of something that *did* work – a sinister quotation from an advertisement in a national newspaper of 1979, in connection with the recent bankruptcy of another paper:

'To the witches of Crows-an-Wra, Carn Brea, Rough Tor and Brent Tor, Dunkery, and the three ladies of Dartmoor Forest. Sincere thanks and congratulations for the successful end to your three years of unrelenting rituals.'

Clearly, the witches of the West Country, unrecognised, and all but invisible, are still going about their age-old business.

Bibliography

The Folklore of Devon, R. Whitlock (Batsford, 1977)

Devon Villages, S.H. Burton (Robert Hale, 1973)

The Devil in Devon, J.R. Coxhead (West Country Handbooks, 1967)

Sketches of Bovey Tracey and District, M.A. Hole (Basil Blackwell, 1930)

Devon Anthology, Jack Simmons (MacMillan, 1971)

Exmoor Wanderings, Eric R. Delderfield (Red Publications, 1956)

Exmoor, S.H. Burton (Robert Hale, 1969/1974)

Dartmoor, Crispin Gill (David & Charles, 1976)

The Devon and Somerset Blackdowns, Ronald Webber (Robert Hale, 1976)

The Stone People, Elizabeth Renier (Hamish Hamilton, 1978)

Devonshire Characters, Rev. S. Baring-Gould (1908)

Nummits and Crummits, Sarah Hewett, 1900 (EP Publishing, 1976)

The Cream of Devon (Devon Federation of Women's Institutes, 1980)

Raleigh Country, E.R. Delderfield (Raleigh Press)

Around and About the Haldon Hills, Chips Barber (Obelisk, 1982)

Playbill, Harvey Crane (Macdonald & Evans, 1980)

100 Years on Dartmoor, William Crossing (David & Charles, 1974)

Dartmoor, D. St. Leger-Gordon (Collins, 1953)

High Dartmoor, Eric Hemery (Robert Hale, 1983)

The Dartmoor Worker, William Crossing (David & Charles, 1966)

BIBLIOGRAPHY

The Dartmoor Magazine, John Shakespeare (1987), Ann Riddon (1987), Paul Rendell (1990), Anne Swinscow (1986, 1987)

Revolt in the West, John Sturt (Devon Books, 1988)

Tudor Cornwall, A.L. Rowse (1941)

The Templer Way, Derek Beavis (Obelisk, 1992)

The North Devon Coast, S.H. Burton (Werner Laurie, 1953)

Folklore and Customs of Rural England, M. Baker (David & Charles, 1974)

Life in a Devon Village, Henry Williamson (Faber & Faber, 1945)

Tales of a Dartmoor Village, Theo Brown (West Country Folklore, 1973)

Legends of Exmoor, Jack Hurley (Exmoor Press, 1973)

Francis Drake, Neville Williams (Weidenfeld & Nicholson, 1973)

The Incredible Armada, James Mildren (Devon Books, 1988)

Sea Stories of Devon, Sarah Foot (Bossiney, 1984)

A Calendar of Country Customs, Ralph Whitlock (Batsford, 1978)

The Land that Changed its Face, Grace Bradbeer (David & Charles, 1973)

Rainbow in the Morning, Eileen Stafford (Headline, 1993)

An Angel From Your Door, Lois Deacon (United Writers, 1973)

Exeter, Brian Little (Batsford, 1953)

Atmospheric Railways, Chas. Hadfield (David & Charles, 1967)

The Witchcraft and Folklore of Dartmoor, Ruth St. Leger Gordon (1965)

Acknowledgements

The author wishes to thank her family, friends and acquaintancies who have helped in the preparation of this book of yarns. She is grateful to Reverend J Dennis Pickering, Chaplain of the Point-in-View Chapel for permission to quote from the Trustees' Minutes, the tour guide at Chambercombe Manor, the Area Librarian of the North Devon Library and Record Office at Barnstaple, John Hayward for permission to quote from his poems, Dartmoor National Park for information from their archaeologist, Ilsington church for access to the church history, and Elizabeth Renier for allowing the use of her research notes.

Acknowledgement is also gratefully made to the Transactions of The Devonshire Association, in particular to the paper on *The Huguenots of Devon* by Dr. Alison Grant and Robin Gwynn, Vol. 117, 1985, and to several folklore reports by Theo Brown in volumes dating from 1978 to 1983.